Presented to:

_____

By:

_____

On:

_____

This book is dedicated to my wife, Helen,
in honor of all she has done through the years
to bring God's Word to his children.
—RS

To my family now and tomorrow, with love.
—KAM

ACKNOWLEDGMENTS

I would like to express my appreciation to: Kim Childress and Barbara Herndon for seeing the potential of *Bible Gems to Remember Illustrated Bible* and helping others at Zondervan see it too; Andrea Vinley Jewell and Mary Hassinger for their editorial expertise; Joe McCarthy for his wise counsel, support, and prayers; and my many brothers and sisters in Christ who encouraged me and prayed for me as I wrote this book. Thanks to all of you!

ZONDERKIDZ

Bible Gems to Remember Illustrated Bible
Copyright © 2019 by Robin Schmitt
Illustrations © 2019 by Kris Aro McLeod

Requests for information should be addressed to:
Zonderkidz, 3900 Sparks Drive SE, Grand Rapids, Michigan 49546

Hardcover ISBN 978-0-310-74688-1
Ebook ISBN 978-0-310-74704-8

Art direction and design: Kris Nelson/StoryLook Design

Printed in China

19 20 21 22 23 /DSC / 21 20 19 18 17 16 15 14 13 12 11 10 9 8 7 6 5 4 3 2 1

BIBLE GEMS
—TO—
REMEMBER
ILLUSTRATED BIBLE

52 Stories with Easy Bible
Memory in 5 Words or Less

WRITTEN BY ROBIN SCHMITT • ILLUSTRATED BY KRIS ARO MCLEOD

A Note to Parents

Gemstones are very short, very powerful clauses from the Bible. They are no more than five words long, so they are easy to remember. Children can memorize them instantly.

Many people study the Bible intently, digging into verses to find valuable truths. That's what a Gemstone, a Bible Gem, is—a nugget of truth mined from Scripture. Here's an example:

The LORD is good.

This Gem comes from Psalm 34:8, which reads,

> Taste and see that the LORD is good;
> blessed is the one who takes refuge in him.

This book offers a year's worth of inspiring, encouraging Gems like that—one per week—paired with exciting Bible stories to help readers understand the Gems. Children will learn 52 wonderful, pocket-sized truths from God's Word, truths they can carry with them forever. Plus, there are more than 100 extra Gems that complement the main Gemstones. Altogether the *Bible Gems to Remember Illustrated Bible* offers over 150 powerful little truths from God's Word.*

Learning what the Bible says and putting it into practice—at home and everywhere—is one of the best means to build character and faith. With that in mind, here are five beneficial ways for children and their families to use the Gemstones in this book:

---

*Note: Quotation marks have been added to some Gemstones to indicate that Jesus or God spoke the words as opposed to, say, one of the psalmists.

Memorize them.

Think about them.

Talk about them.

Pray about them.

Live them out.

The idea of using Bible Gems to help children treasure God's Word in their minds and hearts was inspired in part by an interesting phrase penned by the apostle Paul. In 1 Corinthians 14:19, Paul wrote about speaking five clear words of instruction. Can you imagine what he would say in five words or less to teach children a valuable truth?

Perhaps something like this:
Overcome evil with good. —Romans 12:21

Parents, here's a great Gemstone for you:
Teach them to your children. —Deuteronomy 11:19

I pray that God will enable children, and the adults who love them, to grasp the truths in these Gems and remember them forever, and that the beauty of these Gems will inspire everyone to dig deeper and deeper into God's Word.

—Robin Schmitt

Trust in God's unfailing love.

—Psalm 52:8

Table of Contents

Everything God created is good.

—1 Timothy 4:4

God Makes the World

Genesis 1:1–2:3

God is a great artist, designer, and builder. He thought of wonderful things to make, like stars and planets, oceans and mountains, animals and birds. He planned what they would look like, where he would put them, and what they could do. And then he created them all perfectly. That all takes a lot of imagination, wisdom, and power.

In the beginning, the Great Artist, Designer, and Builder made the world. And he did an awesome job!

When God started, the earth was covered with water. Darkness was all around it. So on the first day, God said, "I want light. Let it shine!" And sure enough, there was light.

God looked at the light he created, and he said, "This is good."

He put the light on one side and the darkness on the other. He called the light day and the darkness night.

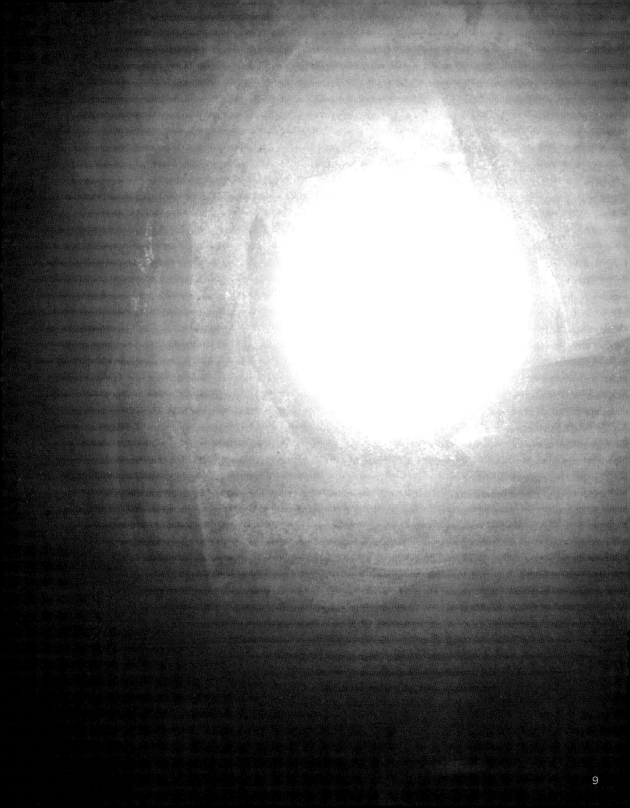

On the second day, God said, "I want something beautiful surrounding the earth. So let blue sky and air cover the world." God changed some of the water to clouds. The water in the clouds floated up in the sky, high above the water below.

On the third day, God said, "I want solid ground." So he gathered the water into pools and let dry ground pop up. God called the pools of water seas, and he called the ground land. He looked at both and said, "This is good too."

Then God said, "Let plants and trees grow on the land." Little green seedlings sprouted everywhere. They grew into short, bushy plants and tall, leafy trees. God looked them over and smiled. "Good, good."

On the fourth day, God said, "I want a sun and a moon and stars. So let them take shape." God looked at the blazing sun, the glowing moon, and the twinkling stars, and he was pleased with his work. "This is good."

But God wanted more on the earth than just plants and trees. So on the fifth day, God said, "I want the seas and the sky to be filled with living things. Let fish and other creatures start swimming. Let all kinds of birds start to fly." Big fish and little fish, sea horses and octopuses, dolphins and whales began moving through the water. Eagles soared above the mountains, and parrots flew in the rain forests. Watching them, God said, "Oh, this is good!"

MORE GEMS

God created
the world.
—Mark 13:19

He made
the universe.
—Hebrews 1:2

We are God's handiwork.

—Ephesians 2:10

God Makes People

Genesis 2:4—25

On the sixth day, God still wasn't done making the world.
Not yet!
God said, "I want animals. So I'll make all kinds of them!"
Elephants trumpeted, horses whinnied, lions roared. Furry
mammals, scaly reptiles, and shiny bugs began running and crawling
and skittering about. Two tigers chased each other, and a wolf
howled just for fun, while cows and sheep munched grass. God
looked at every creature he had made. "Good. This is good," he said.

Then God made his most important creation of all. They were different from everything else God made. He created a man and a woman—Adam and Eve.

What was different about these two? First, God didn't just say, "Let there be people." God formed Adam from the rich soil where the plants and trees grew. Then he blew his own breath into Adam to give him life. Later, God put Adam into a deep sleep, took one of Adam's rib bones, and used it to form Eve.

God made them to be like him in many ways. They could feel love and joy, like God does. And they could think and create things—like using a stick to make a tool or using some flowers to make a bouquet.

When God made Adam and Eve, he used his own hands to form them. His "hands" did the "work," so human beings are God's handiwork. This makes us very special.

God loved Adam and Eve. "Have children!" he told them. "They'll grow up and have children, and their children will have children. I want your family to spread out and fill up the whole earth." God looked at Adam and Eve and everything else he had created. He was pleased with what he had made. "This is all good," he said. "Yes, very good!"

On the seventh day, God rested—but not because he was tired. God stopped working because he was done. The Great Artist, Designer, and Builder had finished his masterpiece.

MORE GEMS

God created
human beings.

—Deuteronomy 4:32

Your hands
made me.

—Psalm 119:73

19

Trust in the LORD.

—Proverbs 3:5

Adam and Eve Listen to the Wrong Voice

Genesis 2–3

Adam and Eve loved God, and they loved each other. They felt good about themselves too. They were beautiful, they were innocent, and they had nothing to hide.

God had made a garden for them in the land of Eden, and they loved their home. They loved watching the sunrise, swimming in the river, playing with the animals, and walking with God in the cool evening breeze.

God wanted the man and the woman to stay alive forever. So he told them, "You can eat the fruit from any of the trees, except for the one in the middle of the garden. If you eat the fruit from that tree, you'll die."

Adam and Eve were happy to obey God. They had all the food they needed. So they stayed away from the deadly tree.

For a while.

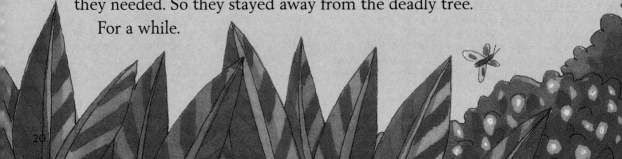

One day, a snake slithered up to Eve.

"Did God really tell you not to eat any fruit from these trees?" it asked.

Eve didn't know the snake was Satan, God's enemy, in disguise. And she didn't know Satan wanted to ruin everything God had created.

"No," Eve said. "God said we could eat fruit from any tree except the one in the middle of the garden. That fruit will kill us."

The snake flicked its tongue. "No, it won't. It will make you wise, just like God!"

Now Eve was confused. Who should she believe, the snake or God?

Eve walked to the middle of the garden. Adam followed her. Staring at the fruit on the tree, Eve thought, *It doesn't look bad. Maybe it really will make me as wise as God.*

She picked some fruit and ate it. Then she gave some to Adam, and he ate it too.

Suddenly, they didn't feel good anymore. They wanted to cover themselves. So they sewed together some leaves to make clothes. But it didn't help much. They still felt bad.

That evening, they heard God walking toward them. They were afraid, so they hid in the trees.

God called, "Where are you?" At first they didn't reply. Finally, Adam answered God, and they came out of their hiding place.

God asked them what happened. They told him they had eaten the deadly fruit.

"It was Eve's fault," Adam said. "She gave some to me."

"It was the snake's fault," Eve said. "He lied to me."

But they both knew they had done something foolish and wrong. If only they had trusted God and obeyed him!

With a sad voice, God told them they couldn't live in the garden anymore. They had to leave. Life outside the garden would be much harder. And one day they would die, just as he warned them.

God still loved Adam and Eve very much. He showed them his love by making better clothes for them before they left. And even though they couldn't be close to him anymore, God kept watching over them.

Do what is right.

—Genesis 4:7

Cain Gets Angry and Jealous

Genesis 4:1-16

Adam and Eve made a new home in the land outside the garden. It wasn't nearly as nice. Thorny weeds came up when they tried to grow food. The animals weren't always friendly like they used to be. One good thing happened, though—Adam and Eve had two sons.

Cain became a farmer. He plowed the ground, planted seeds, and pulled weeds so his plants would be big and strong. Abel became a shepherd. He tended his sheep, feeding them and protecting them from lions and wolves.

The time came to make an offering to God, as a way to worship and thank him. Abel offered the first sheep born from his flock to God. God was pleased with Abel's offering, and he accepted it. Cain offered some of his crops, but he did not offer the first or the best. This didn't please God.

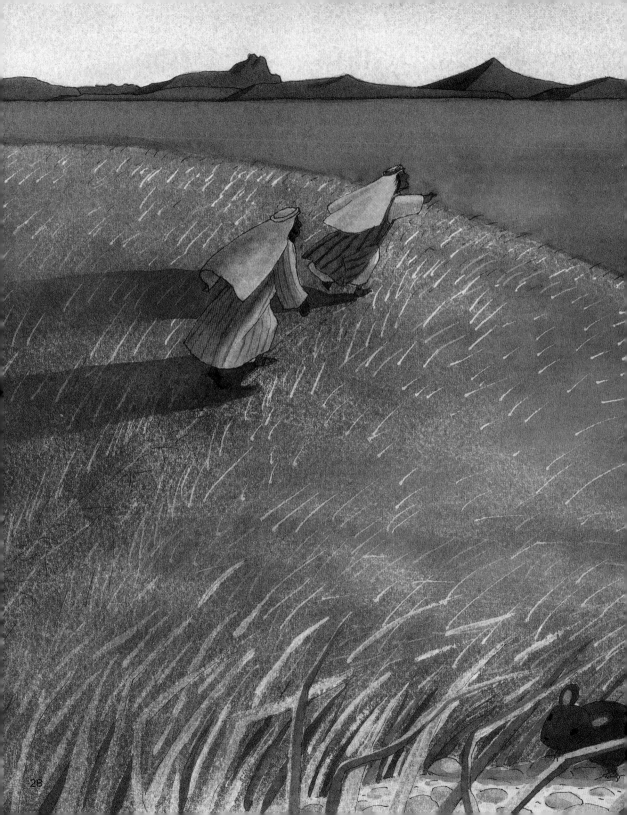

Cain walked away mad.

"Why are you angry?" God asked him. "If you do what is right, I will be pleased with you and bless you."

Cain wouldn't listen to God. Instead, Cain made things worse.

Cain was jealous of Abel because God had accepted Abel's offering but not his. So Cain went to his brother, who was watching the sheep. "Come out to the field with me," Cain said. "I want to show you something."

"What is it?" Abel asked, following him.

"You'll see."

Cain led Abel far into the field, where nobody could see them. Then, with no warning, he attacked Abel and killed him.

Cain thought no one knew what he had done. But God knew.

God told Cain, "Because you killed your brother Abel, from now on you'll wander around the world, without a home. When you plant seeds in the ground, you won't get any crops at all."

Cain had to leave the land he knew, and that made him sad.

Adam and Eve were very sad. One of their sons was dead, and the other was gone. They remembered how terrible they felt when they disobeyed God and had to leave the garden. How they wished Cain had done the right thing!

God was kind to Adam and Eve once more. In time, he gave them another son, a boy named Seth. And even though their sadness over Cain and Abel never went away, they had a reason to be happy again.

MORE GEMS

Pursue righteousness.
—1 Timothy 6:11

Turn from evil.
—Psalm 34:14

Learn to do right.
—Isaiah 1:17

Listen and obey.

—Deuteronomy 5:27

Noah Follows God's Instructions

Genesis 6:1–9:17

God had made Adam and Eve good, but when Adam and Eve disobeyed God in the garden, something inside them changed. Their hearts became sinful, which made it even harder for them to obey God.

Adam and Eve had many more children, and they had sin in their hearts too. Those children grew up and had children of their own. Over time the world filled up with people who could have obeyed God but didn't. Men and women were lying, stealing, and hurting each other. No one was listening to God.

Except Noah.

Noah was a good man. He had a sinful heart, just like everyone else, but he chose to listen to God's commands and obey them.

God was happy with Noah, but he was angry with everyone else. He told Noah, "I'm going to flood the earth and destroy everything on it. But I'll rescue you and your family."

So God told Noah to build a large
boat called an ark. It had to be big enough
to hold Noah and his wife, Noah's sons and
their wives, and two of every kind of animal
and bird. Plus food for everyone.

Noah didn't argue or complain. He obeyed and
started building the boat. It took a long time.

At last the boat was finished. God told Noah, "Get your
family and all the animals inside." Noah obeyed, and God shut the
huge door.

Dark clouds gathered, and it began to rain. Not just a sprinkle—it
poured! The rivers and lakes overflowed, and the waters rose, until
even the mountaintops were underwater.

But everyone inside the boat was safe. God rescued them all
because Noah was faithful.

After forty days, the rain stopped. The boat floated on the water for months.

The people and animals couldn't get out of the boat yet. But they had food to eat, they had each other, and God was watching over them.

Then the water started to go down. After a while, the boat landed on top of a mountain. And when the earth was dry, God told Noah to bring his family and the animals out of the boat.

MORE GEMS

Fully obey
the LORD.
—Deuteronomy 28:1

Listen to
his voice.
—Deuteronomy 30:20

Walk in
obedience.
—Deuteronomy 10:12

Noah was happy to listen and obey. When everyone was out, he worshiped God and thanked him for saving them.

God was pleased, and he made a promise to Noah, his family, and everyone who would live after them—including us. God said, "I will never again destroy the world with a flood."

Then God put a rainbow in the sky as a reminder of his promise.

Be faithful.

—Revelation 2:10

Job Stays Loyal to God

Job 1:1–22

After the flood, the world began to fill up with people again. One of those people was Job. He was a good man, faithful and loyal to God. Job had lots of animals and servants. He had many sons and daughters, who were all grown up and had homes of their own. Job was the richest, most blessed man around.

God's enemy, Satan, didn't like Job. Satan thought that if he could take away all the good things in Job's life, Job would curse God. God knew better, so he let Satan test Job.

One day, thieves stole all of Job's oxen, donkeys, and camels. Then lightning killed all his sheep. Most of his servants died too. And a windstorm killed his sons and daughters.

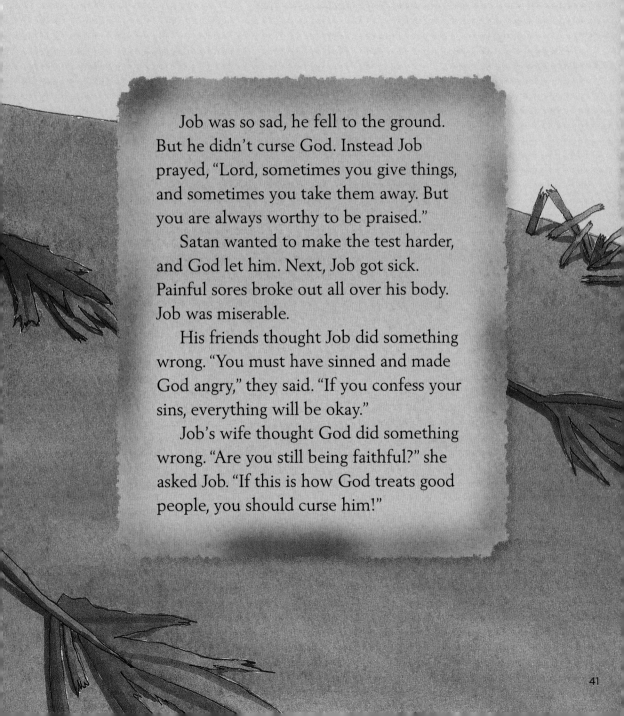

Job was so sad, he fell to the ground. But he didn't curse God. Instead Job prayed, "Lord, sometimes you give things, and sometimes you take them away. But you are always worthy to be praised."

Satan wanted to make the test harder, and God let him. Next, Job got sick. Painful sores broke out all over his body. Job was miserable.

His friends thought Job did something wrong. "You must have sinned and made God angry," they said. "If you confess your sins, everything will be okay."

Job's wife thought God did something wrong. "Are you still being faithful?" she asked Job. "If this is how God treats good people, you should curse him!"

Job didn't know why all the bad things happened. But he knew two important facts. First, Job knew he was a good man. He always honored God and obeyed him. Second, Job knew God was loving and good, and everything God did was right.

Job had always praised God when times were good, and he kept praising God when times got bad. Through it all, Job trusted God and stayed loyal to him.

Job asked God for answers, but Job never cursed God.

And guess what! God talked with Job and honored Job's faithfulness. He knew Job was a good man, and he blessed Job's life again. God made him a rich man once more and gave Job twice as many animals. He gave Job many children and grandchildren. Job lived a long time after that, and he was very happy.

MORE GEMS

Be devoted
to the Lord.
—1 Corinthians 7:34

I am faithful
to you.
—Psalm 86:2

Live by faith.

—Romans 1:17

Abraham Leaves His Home

Genesis 12–25

God had a plan to make the world perfect again. He chose a man named Abraham to play a big part in that plan. But first Abraham would have to trust God and do something a little scary.

God told Abraham, "Leave the country you're living in now. Follow me, and I'll show you a new land."

The Lord made a special promise to Abraham. "I'll make you into a great nation," God said. "You'll be important and famous. I'll bless your friends and curse your enemies, and through you I'll bless the world."

Abraham was amazed. He and his wife, Sarah, were old, and they had never been able to have children. God was saying they were going to have a child, and then grandchildren, and then great-grandchildren. Abraham's family was going to grow so big that they would form their own country!

Now Abraham had to make a choice. Would he stay where he was, or would he believe God and go?

Abraham decided to pack up everything he owned. Then he left his home and set out for the new land. He took his wife Sarah, his nephew Lot, his servants, and all of his animals. Abraham would live by faith, following God wherever God led him.

After a long journey, they made it to a land called Canaan.

God was pleased with Abraham. He told him, "I will give this land to you, your children, your grandchildren, and everyone who comes after you."

Abraham was so happy. Canaan had big, wide fields for raising cows and sheep, and the soil was good for growing fruits and vegetables. Abraham was glad he had chosen to trust God and follow him. He built an altar and praised God.

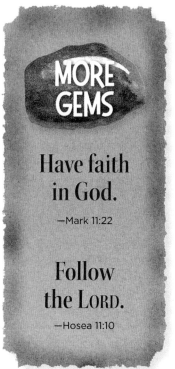

Years later, God rewarded Abraham again for his faith by giving him and his wife a child. Abraham looked at all the land around him, and all the animals and crops in the fields. Holding Isaac, his newborn son, Abraham thought about all the grandchildren and great-grandchildren God had promised him. Abraham knew God was going to use his family to bless the whole world.

The LORD will guide you.

—Isaiah 58:11

God Gives Isaac a Wife

Genesis 24

When Isaac was all grown up, Abraham called his most trusted servant. "My son needs a wife," Abraham said. "I want you to find one for him."

Abraham told his servant, "Don't let Isaac marry a woman who lives in Canaan. The people here don't know God, and they don't follow God's ways. Go back to the country I came from. One of my relatives there can be Isaac's wife. God will help you find the right woman."

The servant loaded ten camels with jewelry and fancy clothes. Traveling far, the servant and his men reached the town of Nahor. They stopped at the well outside of town. The camels kneeled down to rest.

Then the servant prayed, "Lord, this is where the young women come for water. Please guide me to the one who will make a good wife for Isaac. I'll ask each young woman for a drink. If one of them gives water to me and to the camels, I'll know she's the one."

As the servant was praying, a beautiful young woman came to the well. Her name was Rebekah, and she carried a jar on her shoulder. The servant asked her for a drink. "Yes, of course," she said. She poured him some water, then gave some to the camels.

The servant was excited. He gave Rebekah some jewelry and asked about her family. She told him who her father and grandfather were. Rebekah was one of Abraham's relatives!

Bowing to worship God, the servant said, "Thank you, Lord. You answered my prayer—even before I finished praying!"

Rebekah ran home and told her family about the servant of Abraham. Her brother, Laban, invited the servant and his men to stay at their home. There the servant gave Rebekah more jewelry and some clothes. Then he told her family he had come to find a wife for Isaac. Rebekah's father agreed to let Rebekah become Isaac's wife. Rebekah's mother asked her, "Will you go with Abraham's servant and marry Isaac?"

Rebekah thought for a moment. Then she said, "Yes, I will."

The next day, Rebekah got on a camel and followed the servant on the long trip to Canaan. When they arrived, Rebekah saw a man walking toward her. "That's Isaac," the servant said. Climbing off the camel, Rebekah went to meet Isaac.

Isaac and Rebekah were married, and they loved each other. In time, they had children, twin baby boys. And God promised the same thing to Isaac that he had promised Abraham. God would give the land of Canaan to Abraham's family, make them into a great nation, and bless the whole world through them.

MORE GEMS

Ask God for help.
—1 Timothy 5:5

The Lord is my helper.
—Hebrews 13:6

Show me the way.
—Psalm 143:8

Commit yourselves to the LORD.

—1 Samuel 7:3

Jacob Makes a Promise to God

Genesis 28

Isaac and Rebekah's sons grew up, and they lived with their parents in Canaan. Some twins are exactly alike, but these twins were not.

Esau had red hair, and not just on his head—he was hairy all over. He liked roaming outdoors, and he liked to hunt. Jacob had dark hair on his head, but the rest of his body was smooth. He liked to stay home, and he liked to cook.

Since they were twins, Esau and Jacob were the same age. But Esau had been born just before Jacob. That made Esau the firstborn son, which meant he would get a special blessing from his father one day.

Jacob wanted that blessing for himself! And his mother believed God really wanted Jacob to have it. So Rebekah made a plan to help Jacob steal Esau's blessing.

Isaac had grown old, and he couldn't see
anymore. Rebekah dressed Jacob in Esau's clothes, so he
would smell like Esau. She even put goatskins on Jacob's hands, so
they would feel hairy like Esau's.

The plan worked! Isaac was fooled, and he gave Jacob the
blessing.

Esau was angry enough to kill his brother. Rebekah told Jacob,
"Run away to your uncle Laban until Esau calms down."

Jacob set out on the journey. That night, he slept on the ground,
using a stone for a pillow. Jacob dreamed of a stairway that went to

heaven. Angels were walking up and down on it,
and God was at the top.

God appeared to Jacob in this dream for a special reason. "I am
the Lord," he told Jacob. "I am the God of your grandfather and
your father." He wanted to be Jacob's God too. So he gave Jacob the
same promise he had given Abraham and Isaac—that he would give
Canaan to Abraham's family, make them into a great nation, and
bless the world through them.

"I'll be with you, Jacob, and I'll watch over you," God said. "I'll
bring you safely home. Don't worry, I won't leave you."

When Jacob woke up, he knew he had met God. "This is God's house!" he said. "This is the gateway to heaven!" He named the place Bethel, which means "house of God."

Then Jacob made a promise to God. "Lord, you are the God of my father and my grandfather," he said. "If you will stay with me and watch over me, like you promised, then you will be my God too."

From that day on, Jacob and God had a special relationship. Jacob had committed himself to the Lord. Now they belonged to each other, like a father and a son.

MORE GEMS

LORD, you are my God.
—Isaiah 25:1

I belong to the LORD.
—Isaiah 44:5

Do not give up.

—Galatians 6:9

Jacob Clings to God

Genesis 32

Jacob went to live with his uncle Laban. When Jacob saw Laban's daughter Rachel, he fell in love. So Jacob and Laban made a deal. Jacob promised to work for Laban for seven years, and Laban promised to let Jacob marry Rachel after that.

But when seven years passed, Laban tricked Jacob—just like Jacob had tricked his father. Laban gave his daughter Leah to Jacob instead. When Jacob complained, Laban said, "Leah is older, so she had to get married first. If you promise to work for me seven more years, you can marry Rachel too." (In those times, men sometimes had more than one wife.)

So Jacob had two wives. And before long, he had eleven sons and a daughter. It was a big family! Jacob was happy.

Except for one problem.

His uncle Laban was always trying to trick him. First he told Jacob, "All the newborn animals with spots will be yours." That seemed fair to Jacob. But all the baby animals had spots. Laban didn't want to give Jacob all the animals, so Laban changed his mind. "All the ones with stripes will be yours," he said. Then they all had stripes!

God was blessing Jacob by giving him lots of animals and making him rich. Laban was very angry about that!

So God told Jacob it was time to go back to Canaan. Jacob gathered his family and his animals and headed back home.

But soon Jacob had another problem.

He heard that his brother, Esau, was coming to meet him—with four hundred men! Jacob thought, Esau must still be angry that I stole his blessing. His army will attack us and kill us all. So Jacob prayed to God for help.

At the Jabbok River, Jacob sent everyone across. But Jacob didn't cross the river. He spent the night beside it, alone. There a man appeared and started wrestling with Jacob. Jacob was scared and confused, but somehow he knew this man was special—maybe an angel sent from heaven. Jacob believed this man could bless him and save him and his family from Esau. So Jacob wouldn't let go.

Finally, the man said, "Let me go. It's morning, and the sun is rising."

"Not unless you bless me," Jacob replied.

And the man did. But first he changed Jacob's name to Israel, which means "he struggles with God." The man told Jacob, "You struggled with God, and you didn't quit. You won your struggle." That's when Jacob realized the man was really God!

Later, God helped Esau calm down. When Esau saw Jacob, he was happy. He ran and hugged Jacob. They both cried tears of joy.

From that time on, Jacob's name was Israel. Why? Because he didn't give up. He held on to God with all his might. He kept his faith in God.

MORE GEMS

You need
to persevere.
—Hebrews 10:36

Hold fast
to the Lord.
—Joshua 23:8

God will be with you.

—Joshua 1:9

God Stays with Joseph

Genesis 37–41

Israel took his family to Canaan, and there Rachel had a baby, named Joseph. Now Israel had twelve sons. God was making Abraham's family into a nation, just like he promised.

Israel loved his son Joseph the most, and he gave him a special robe to wear. Joseph's brothers were jealous and hated Joseph.

When Joseph was seventeen, God showed him something wonderful in a dream. Joseph described the dream to his brothers. "We were gathering wheat in the field," he said. "My bundle stood up, and yours bowed down."

The brothers were angry. "Do you think we'll bow down to you?" they asked.

God gave Joseph another dream. "I saw the sun, the moon, and eleven stars," Joseph told his brothers. "They all bowed down to me."

Now his brothers hated him even more. Joseph seemed to think the whole family would bow down to him, even his mother and father!

One day, while the brothers were tending sheep, they saw Joseph coming. "Let's kill him!" said one brother. But the oldest one said, "No, let's throw him in this deep hole instead."

So the brothers grabbed Joseph, took his special robe, and threw him in.

When Joseph's brothers saw some traders passing by with their camels, the brothers had an idea. They pulled Joseph out of the hole and sold him for a few pieces of silver. The traders took Joseph to Egypt as a slave.

Joseph had to work hard. But God was with him and helped him do a good job. Joseph's master was so pleased that he put Joseph in charge of his whole house.

Then Joseph was thrown in jail! His master's wife lied, saying Joseph did something wrong. The jail was cold and dark. But God was with Joseph, and he helped Joseph again. The warden liked Joseph and put him in charge of all the prisoners.

And then God did something amazing. Egypt's king had two bad dreams. One of his servants, who had been in prison, remembered Joseph. "Joseph can tell the meaning of dreams," he said. So the king sent for Joseph.

MORE
GEMS

God goes
with you.
—Deuteronomy 31:6

He will never
leave you.
—Deuteronomy 31:8

The LORD
is with me.
—Psalm 118:6

Joseph told the king, "Only God understands dreams, and he told me what yours mean. A famine is coming. Egypt must store up food." The king saw that Joseph was wise. So he put him in charge of everything, to help Egypt get ready for the famine.

What a life Joseph had! First he was a favorite son. Then he was a slave, then a prisoner, and then a powerful ruler. Some times were good, and some were bad. But God was with Joseph through it all.

Forgive one another.

—Colossians 3:13

Joseph Forgives His Brothers

Genesis 42–50

Joseph's brothers had never told their father, Israel, what they did to his favorite son. They let him think for many years that a wild animal had killed Joseph.

Then the famine came. No food would grow anywhere in the world. But Israel heard that Egypt had stored up food, and people could go there to buy some. He told his sons, "Go to Egypt and buy food for us before we starve."

So Joseph's brothers traveled to Egypt. They went to the man selling food. He was a powerful ruler. The king of Egypt had put him in charge of everything. The brothers bowed down to him.

They didn't know it was Joseph all grown up.

But Joseph knew these men were his brothers. He remembered his dreams about them bowing down to him. The dreams had come true.

At first, Joseph was happy to see his brothers again. But then he recalled how they treated him. They had thrown him into a pit and sold him to strangers. Joseph loved his brothers, but he was angry. He didn't know whether to hug them or hurt them.

For now, he pretended not to know them. And he decided to test them.

"You're all spies!" he said, to see what they would do.

"No, no, we're not spies," they replied. "We've come to buy food."

Then in their own language, the brothers told each other, "God is paying us back for what we did to Joseph." They didn't think the Egyptian man could understand them. But Joseph could! He knew they were worried and upset. Yet he wondered if they were sorry for what they did.

Joseph sold some food to his brothers and sent them home. But he kept one of them, Simeon, as a prisoner. Later, the brothers came back to Egypt to buy more food and get Simeon out of prison. Joseph kept testing his brothers and watching them. He could tell they were sorry for the way they had treated him. Finally, Joseph couldn't pretend anymore. Weeping with joy, he revealed himself and told his brothers, "It's me, Joseph!"

At first, they were stunned. Then they were scared. If this man really was Joseph, surely he wanted revenge.

But Joseph said, "Don't be afraid. And don't be upset about what you did to me. God used that bad thing in a good way. He made me a ruler in Egypt so I could help people during the famine. God used me to save many lives!"

Joseph hugged his brothers and forgave them.

The king of Egypt told Joseph to invite all of his relatives to come live in Egypt. Then they would be with Joseph and have all the food they needed. "I'll give your people the best land," said the king.

Joseph's brothers went back to Canaan and told their father that Joseph was alive. He was so glad. Israel took all of his sons and daughters and grandchildren—almost seventy people—to Egypt. They lived there happily for the rest of their lives.

MORE GEMS

Forgive everyone who sins.
—Luke 11:4

Love covers over all wrongs.
—Proverbs 10:12

The Lord is powerful.

—Joshua 4:24

God Rescues His People

Exodus 1–15

Israel's family grew bigger and bigger. Many years later, there were almost a million people in it! They still lived in Egypt.

But now the Egyptians had a new king. He had never heard of Joseph.

This king was worried. "What if all these Israelites attack us?" So he made them slaves. He forced them to make bricks and buildings. The slave masters were harsh, and the Israelites had to work very hard.

The people of Israel cried to God for help, and God heard them.

God spoke to Moses, an Israelite who had left Egypt and was tending sheep in the desert. One day, Moses saw a bush that was on fire but wasn't burning up. From the bush, he heard God say, "Go back to Egypt. Tell the king to let my people go."

Moses and his brother Aaron went to the king. When they told the king what God said, the king refused to obey. "I don't know God," he said. "Why should I listen to him?"

God told Aaron to hit the river with Moses's staff. Aaron did, and the water turned into blood. The Egyptians couldn't drink it, and all the fish died.

The king still wouldn't obey.

So God caused more trouble for the Egyptians:

Frogs hopped out of the river and covered Egypt.
Gnats filled the air.
Flies appeared everywhere.
Sickness killed their cows, sheep, and goats.
Painful sores broke out all over the Egyptians.
Hail destroyed half the crops.
Locusts ate the crops that were left.
A deep darkness spread over the land.

But the king still refused to obey God.
Finally, God sent an angel to kill the firstborn son in every Egyptian home.
The king had seen enough. He told Moses, "Take all the Israelites and leave!"

The Israelites hurried out of Egypt with their families and their animals. God led them with a pillar of cloud by day and a pillar of fire by night. Soon they reached the Red Sea.

And then the king of Egypt changed his mind. "I want my slaves back!" Climbing into his chariot, he led his army out to chase the Israelites.

As the army approached, God told Moses, "Hold up your staff and split the sea in two. Then my people can walk through it."

Moses raised his staff. God blew a strong wind and divided the water, making a dry path in the middle.

The Israelites rushed down the path. The Egyptian soldiers charged after them.

When the Israelites had crossed the sea, Moses raised his staff again. The water fell on the Egyptians. The army was gone!

Shouting with joy, God's people celebrated. Far from Egypt, safe and free, Moses and the Israelites sang about how powerful God was.

MORE GEMS

God is mighty.
—Job 36:5

The LORD is a warrior.
—Exodus 15:3

The LORD will deliver us.
—Isaiah 36:18

The Lord Will Provide.

—Genesis 22:14

God Feeds His People in the Desert

Exodus 16–17

From the shore of the Red Sea, God led the Israelites into the desert.

Walking in the desert was hot. It made the people tired and cranky. Not only that, but soon their food was gone. The people started complaining.

"What are we going to eat?"

"We need food!"

"Our animals are hungry too."

Moses told God what the people were saying. God said, "Tomorrow morning, I'll give you bread from heaven. But I'm going to test the people to see if they'll do what I say."

So Moses and Aaron told the Israelites, "God heard your complaints. When you wake up tomorrow, you'll have all the bread you need. The Lord will provide it for you. Then you'll know that he is the one true God."

The next morning, when the people came out of their tents, dew was all around the camp.

"Where's the bread?" they wondered.

As the sun rose, the dew dried up. The sand was covered with thin, white flakes.

"What's that?" the people asked.

Moses said, "It's the bread God promised. Fill a jar with it for each person in your tent. Take only as much as you need for one day. God wants you to gather it each morning. On the seventh day of every week, do not go out to gather any. Instead you must rest."

A man asked, "What are we supposed to eat that day?"

"On the sixth day, fill two jars for each person," Moses said. "Then you'll have enough to eat for two days."

The people started filling jars with the flakes. A boy tried one. He told his mother, "It tastes like honey!"

A few people kept some bread overnight, so they wouldn't have to gather food the next day. In the morning, the leftover bread looked and smelled bad. They couldn't eat it.

Moses was angry and told them they needed to obey God's instructions.

Each morning, the bread appeared. On the sixth day, Moses reminded the people to gather twice as much.

A woman asked, "If we keep some until morning, won't it go bad?"

"Watch and see!" Moses replied.

On the seventh day, the people woke up hungry. They peered into their jars, and the leftover bread looked fresh. It smelled wonderful, and it tasted good.

Some greedy Israelites went out that morning looking for more. This time, God was angry. He told Moses, "I want all of you to obey my commands. I've given you all the food you need. But the seventh day is a special day to rest."

From then on, all the people rested on the seventh day, every week. They obeyed God, thankful that he was such a good provider.

Obey the LORD's commands.

—Judges 3:4

God Gives His People Some Rules

Exodus 19:1–20:21; 24:12–18; 31:18; 32:1–34:28

God led the Israelites to a mountain in the desert called Mount Sinai. He wanted to have a special meeting there with Moses and the people.

The Israelites set up camp, then got ready for the meeting. When the time came, they gathered at the bottom of the mountain. God appeared at the top in a thick, dark cloud. Lightning flashed and thunder boomed. Fire blazed, smoke billowed, and a trumpet blast grew louder and louder.

The people were afraid.

"Please, go talk to God for us!" they begged Moses. "Then come back and tell us what he says. We'll listen and obey."

Moses said, "Don't worry. It's okay. God is showing you his power so you will respect and obey him."

Moses went up on Mount Sinai and stayed there for forty days. During that time, God wrote ten rules on two stone tablets and told Moses to give them to the Israelites.

Don't worship other gods.

Don't make statues of gods and worship them.

Don't misuse God's name.

Rest on the seventh day of every week.

Honor your parents.

Those were good rules, because they would protect the Israelites and help them treat each other well. Moses was glad to take the rules back to the people. But when he came down from the mountain, Moses saw a sad sight. The people were already disobeying one of God's rules. They had made a gold statue of a cow and were worshiping it.

Moses was upset. He threw down the stone tablets, shattering them. He destroyed the statue and told the Israelites, "You've sinned badly!" Then he went back up the mountain and asked God to forgive them.

God was angry. But Moses prayed for the people, and God did not destroy them. He didn't leave them either. He gave them another chance to do what is right. Moses made new stone tablets, so the people would remember God's commands and obey them.

MORE GEMS

Listen to the LORD's instruction.

—Isaiah 30:9

Walk in obedience to him.

—Deuteronomy 30:16

Keep his commands.

—Deuteronomy 30:16

Remember the miracles.

—Nehemiah 9:17

Joshua Sets Up a Reminder

Joshua 3–4

The time came for the Israelites to enter the land God promised Abraham and his family.

After Moses died, God chose Joshua to be the new leader. God told Joshua, "Be strong! Be brave! I'll be with you, just like I was with Moses."

So Joshua told everyone to get ready to cross the Jordan River. The water was deep and flowing fast, and the people wondered how they would get across.

Joshua knew what to do; God had given him instructions. Joshua ordered the priests to get the special wood box covered in gold called the ark. Inside the ark were the two stone tablets with God's rules written on them. "Take the ark to the river," Joshua said. "Then step into the water."

Joshua told the people, "God is going to do something amazing. When you see it, you'll know he is with us. He will get us safely across the river, and he will take us to our new home!"

99

The priests carried the ark on two long poles toward the river. As soon as their feet touched the water, the river began to dry up!

The water got lower and lower until it was gone. The priests carried the ark to the middle of the riverbed, then stood there on dry ground.

The people hurried across. They were laughing, shouting, and praising God as they helped each other along.

God told Joshua, "Choose twelve men. Have them pick up twelve big stones from the middle of the riverbed and bring them here. Then stack up the stones. The pile of stones will help everyone remember what happened today."

Joshua did what God said. Each man picked up a stone and carried it out on his shoulder, and Joshua piled them up.

After that, the priests carried the ark to the other side of the river. As the last priest stepped out, the water began flowing again. The river filled up, as high as before.

Then Joshua spoke to the people. "This pile of stones will be a reminder forever," he said. "Someday your children will ask you what it means. Tell them about the miracle God performed. When you look at these stones, remember that God is powerful. Remember to respect him. Remember to serve him."

The Lord gives strength.

—Psalm 29:11

God Gives Samson Power

Judges 13–16

With Joshua leading them, the Israelites moved into the Promised Land.

But after Joshua died, the Israelites forgot God and started worshiping the statues of the Canaanite gods. The Lord would punish the Israelites by letting their enemies bully them. Then God's people would cry out for help, and God would bring a hero to rescue them.

One of God's heroes was Samson. God chose Samson before he was born. God sent an angel to visit an Israelite man and his wife who had not been able to have children. The angel told them they were going to have a son.

"As a sign that he belongs to God, don't cut his hair," the angel said. "He will rescue God's people from their enemies, the Philistines."

When Samson was born, his parents were happy. They didn't cut his hair while he was growing up. And when Samson was a man, he didn't cut his hair either. He stayed faithful to God, and God made him the strongest man around.

Samson was so strong that when he was tied up, he broke the thick ropes. And when he was trapped in a city, he crashed through the city's huge gate and carried the doors away with him!

One day, a group of
Philistines made Samson
angry, so he fought them.
Then an army of Philistines
attacked Samson, and he
defeated them too. This
made the leaders of the
Philistines angry. They
wanted to get even.

So they found a way to capture Samson.
They paid a woman named Delilah to
trick him into telling her the secret of his
strength. After she begged and begged,
Samson said, "I belong to God in a special
way, so my hair has never been cut. If I cut
my hair, all my strength will go away."

While Samson was asleep, Delilah
had someone shave off his hair. Then the
Philistines hiding in the room grabbed
Samson and tied him up. Samson was weak;
he couldn't break the ropes. The Philistines
blinded Samson, took him away, and made
him a slave.

But his hair began to grow back.

One day, the Philistines took Samson to the temple of their god. They wanted to thank their god for giving them victory over Samson. They made Samson perform for them. After that, he asked a servant to lead him to the pillars so he could lean on them and rest. Feeling the pillars with his hands, Samson whispered, "Lord, give me strength again, so I can defeat these Philistines one more time!"

With his right hand on one pillar and his left hand on another, Samson pushed as hard as he could. He was strong again! The pillars toppled, and the roof of the temple came down. The whole temple was destroyed, along with everyone in it. As he died, Samson won his greatest victory.

Samson wasn't perfect, but he was one of God's heroes. When he needed strength, he called on God, and God gave him the power to save his people.

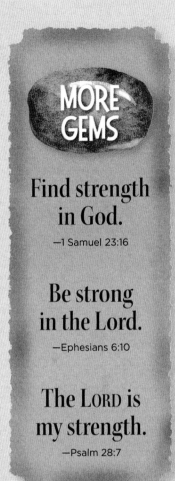

MORE GEMS

Find strength in God.
—1 Samuel 23:16

Be strong in the Lord.
—Ephesians 6:10

The LORD is my strength.
—Psalm 28:7

Love the Lord.

—Deuteronomy 6:5

God Chooses David to Be King

1 Samuel 8–10; 15; 16:1–13

Samuel was a prophet, one of God's messengers. God spoke to Samuel, and Samuel told the Israelites what God wanted them to do.

When Samuel grew old, the people asked for a king. This upset Samuel, because God was their King. Samuel warned the people that they were making a mistake. But they wouldn't listen. So God told Samuel to give them what they wanted.

God chose a man named Saul to be king. Samuel poured oil on Saul's head as a sign that God had chosen him. Then Samuel brought Saul in front of the people, saying, "God has given you this man to be your king."

Everyone cheered, shouting, "Long live the king!"

Saul was a good king for a while, but then he started ignoring Samuel and God. He didn't love God enough to obey him. So God rejected Saul. He was still the king, but God wasn't with him anymore.

God told Samuel to go to the town of Bethlehem to choose a new king. "A man named Jesse lives in that town," God said. "One of his sons loves me. He will do everything I ask him to do."

So Samuel went to Bethlehem. He invited Jesse and his sons to a special meal. Samuel saw Jesse's oldest son and thought, *This man is tall and handsome. God must have chosen him.* But God told Samuel, "He's not the one. I don't want someone who just looks good. I want someone with a good heart."

Jesse showed seven of his sons to Samuel. But God didn't choose any of them. Samuel asked Jesse, "Do you have any other sons?"

"I have one more, my youngest," Jesse said. "His name is David. He's taking care of the sheep."

Samuel told Jesse to send for him.

113

David loved the Lord. He yearned to be near God. He prayed to him. He wrote praises, called psalms, to sing to him. And most important of all, he did everything God wanted him to do.

When a servant ran up, David asked, "What's going on?"

"I don't know," the servant said. "But your father wants to see you. Go! I'll watch the sheep while you're gone."

As soon as Samuel saw David, God told him, "He's the one. Pour oil on his head to show that I've chosen him. David loves me. He will be the new king!"

MORE GEMS

I love you, LORD.
—Psalm 18:1

My spirit longs for you.
—Isaiah 26:9

My soul thirsts for God.
—Psalm 42:2

The battle is the LORD's.

—1 Samuel 17:47

David Defeats Goliath

1 Samuel 17:1–58

The Philistine army came to attack God's people. King Saul led his army out to fight them. The Philistines set up camp on one side of a valley, and the Israelites pitched their tents on the other. In the morning, the two armies formed battle lines.

An enormous Philistine soldier stepped into the valley. His name was Goliath, and he was over nine feet tall. He wore bronze armor and carried a long, heavy spear. A large sword hung from his belt, and a javelin was strapped on his back. A young soldier stood with Goliath, holding the giant's shield.

"I defy the army of Israel!" Goliath shouted. "Send out a man to fight me. If he wins, we'll all be your slaves. But if I win, you'll be our slaves."

None of the Israelites dared to fight him.

The shepherd David was bringing food to three of his brothers, who were Israelite soldiers. David heard Goliath's words.

"Who does he think he is?" David asked the men around him. "Nobody can insult God's army like that!"

One of the soldiers told King Saul what David had said. Saul sent for David. David told the king, "Don't worry about this giant. I'll fight him!"

King Saul was amazed. "You can't," he said. "You're too young, and you've never fought in a battle. Goliath has been a warrior his whole life."

David replied, "I've been a shepherd my whole life, and I've been in plenty of battles. Every time a lion or bear attacked one of the sheep, I fought it and killed it. God protected me from wild animals. He'll protect me from this giant."

So Saul agreed to let David fight Goliath. David picked up his shepherd's staff and sling. Going to a stream, he found five stones and put them in his bag.

When Goliath saw David, he said, "Is this a joke? He's not much more than a boy!"

David pointed at him. "You have a sword, a spear, and a javelin. But I have God! He'll help me beat you, because you're bullying his people. This is God's battle, not mine."

Whirling his sling, David hurled a stone at Goliath. It struck the giant's forehead, and Goliath fell down dead.

The Philistine soldiers panicked and ran away. With a shout, the Israelites charged after them. The Lord gave his people a great victory that day. And it was all because David was brave enough to stand up to evil and trusted God to help him defeat it.

MORE GEMS

The LORD gives victory.
—Psalm 20:6

God will fight for us!
—Nehemiah 4:20

God gives wisdom.

—Ecclesiastes 2:26

Solomon Asks God to Make Him Wise

1 Chronicles 17; 22; 28-29; 2 Chronicles 1; 3; 7; 9; 1 Kings 10

After King Saul died, David became the new king of Israel.

With God's help, David defeated many of the Israelites' enemies and captured many of their cities. He built a beautiful palace in Jerusalem, because that city was where God wanted the people to come worship him. David wanted to build a temple for God there too, but God told him, "I don't want you to build a temple for me. One of your sons will be king after you. I want him to build the temple."

King David didn't argue or complain. Instead, he praised God and thanked him for making him king, blessing his family, and making Israel God's special nation.

David had a son named Solomon. God told David that out of all his sons, Solomon would be the next king. Solomon was the one God had chosen to build the temple.

While Solomon was growing up, King David got everything ready. His people worked with others from nearby nations to cut large stones and chop down trees to make lumber. They gathered all kinds of metal—gold, silver, bronze, and iron. King David made sure Solomon had all he would need to build God's temple.

But Solomon needed something more—not just to build the temple but also to be a good king. Solomon needed wisdom. And only God could give him that!

David told Solomon, "Honor God, and serve him with all your heart. He will give you the wisdom you need."

Soon after Solomon became king, God appeared to him in a dream. God said, "I'll give you anything you ask for."

Solomon thought about it, and then he replied, "Lord, I'm young, and I've never been a king before. Please give me wisdom. That's all I really want."

God was pleased. "Since that is your heart's desire, I will give it to you," he told Solomon. "And because you made such a good choice, I'll also give you riches and honor. You'll be the wisest and richest king ever."

The Lord made Solomon famous all over the world, and leaders of other countries traveled far to hear him speak. King Solomon wrote down many wise sayings called proverbs. And with the wisdom God put in his heart, he ruled Israel justly and fairly. The people were blessed to have such a wise king.

MORE GEMS

Get wisdom, get understanding.
—Proverbs 4:5

Wisdom is better than strength.
—Ecclesiastes 9:16

Gain a heart of wisdom.
—Psalm 90:12

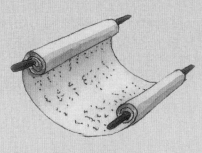

Do not follow other gods.

—Deuteronomy 6:14

Elijah Holds a Contest

1 Kings 18

Elijah was a prophet who loved and served the Lord. The Lord would give him a message, and Elijah would tell the people what the Lord said.

Other prophets worshiped and served a fake god named Baal. They were leading many Israelites to follow Baal instead of the Lord.

But Elijah knew the Lord was the only God that existed, the only God who was real. So Elijah held a contest to prove that the Lord was the one true God.

He told all the Israelites to come to Mount Carmel. He told the prophets of Baal to come too. Everyone gathered on the mountain. Even the king of Israel came.

Elijah was brave. All alone, he faced 450 prophets of Baal. But Elijah had faith in the Lord.

He said to the Israelites, "Some of you think the Lord is God. Others think Baal is the almighty one. If the Lord is the real God, then everyone should worship him. But if Baal is, then we should all worship Baal."

Elijah told the prophets of Baal, "Ask Baal to light a fire, and I'll ask the Lord. Whoever lights a fire is the real God!"

Everyone agreed. The prophets of Baal built an altar, put some wood on it, and started praying to Baal. Nothing happened. They danced around and begged Baal to answer. Still nothing happened.

Elijah picked up twelve stones and built an altar. He gathered some wood and placed it on top. Then he dug a deep trench around the altar and told the Israelites to pour water over everything. "Do it again," he said. And then, "Now do it a third time!" The wood was very wet, and the trench was full of water.

Elijah looked up to heaven and prayed, "Lord, you are the God of Abraham, Isaac, and Israel. Show everyone that you alone are truly God."

Fire shot down from the sky. It burned up the wood. It burned up the altar. It even burned up the water in the trench.

Baal lost the contest. The Lord won.

Amazed, the Israelites all bowed to the ground. Over and over, they cried out, "The Lord is God! The Lord is God!"

MORE GEMS

There is only
one God.
—Romans 3:30

LORD, you
are God!
—2 Samuel 7:28

God is merciful and forgiving.

—Daniel 9:9

Jonah Delivers God's Warning

Jonah 1–4

One day, God spoke to a man named Jonah. God told him, "Go to the city of Nineveh. Tell the people I'm going to destroy them because they are cruel and dishonest and worship false gods."

Jonah didn't want to go. Those people were his enemies! Jonah knew that God is merciful. *If I warn the people of Nineveh, they might stop sinning,* Jonah thought. *They might beg God to forgive them, and then God would! I don't want God to forgive my enemies. I want him to destroy them.*

So Jonah didn't go to Nineveh. Instead, he got on a ship going in the other direction and ran away from God.

God wasn't fooled. He knew right where Jonah was. He knew exactly what Jonah was doing. So God sent a mighty storm to turn Jonah around.

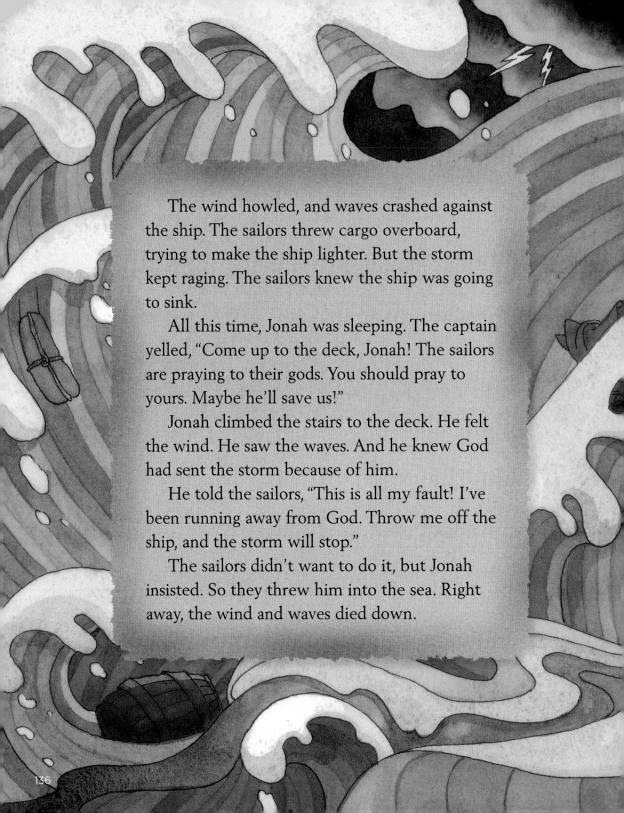

The wind howled, and waves crashed against the ship. The sailors threw cargo overboard, trying to make the ship lighter. But the storm kept raging. The sailors knew the ship was going to sink.

All this time, Jonah was sleeping. The captain yelled, "Come up to the deck, Jonah! The sailors are praying to their gods. You should pray to yours. Maybe he'll save us!"

Jonah climbed the stairs to the deck. He felt the wind. He saw the waves. And he knew God had sent the storm because of him.

He told the sailors, "This is all my fault! I've been running away from God. Throw me off the ship, and the storm will stop."

The sailors didn't want to do it, but Jonah insisted. So they threw him into the sea. Right away, the wind and waves died down.

As Jonah was sinking into the water, he prayed to God for help. God had compassion and sent a giant fish to swallow Jonah and keep him alive.

Inside the fish, Jonah felt sorry for disobeying God. He praised and thanked God for saving his life. God forgave Jonah, and three days later the fish spit up Jonah onto the ground.

Once again, God told Jonah to go to Nineveh. This time, Jonah went.

Jonah walked through the city, warning everyone, "God is going to destroy you because of your sins!"

The people of Nineveh stopped sinning and started praying. They begged God to forgive them. And God did.

Jonah was angry. He told God, "I knew this would happen, because you are merciful and forgiving. That's why I ran away."

Jonah couldn't understand why God would forgive his enemies. They were such bad people! So God tried to explain. He told Jonah, "These people didn't know right from wrong. Now they do. I had compassion on you when you disobeyed me and ran away. They are sorry, and I have compassion on anyone who prays to me and turns from their sin."

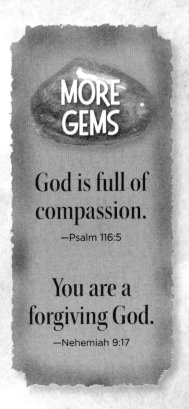

MORE GEMS

God is full of compassion.
—Psalm 116:5

You are a forgiving God.
—Nehemiah 9:17

There is a God.

—Daniel 2:28

God Shows Daniel the King's Dream

Daniel 2

Babylonia was a mighty country, and Nebuchadnezzar was its king. The king and his army broke down the wall around Jerusalem and attacked the Israelites. Entering Jerusalem, they destroyed the temple that had been built for God. Then they captured the people and took them to the city of Babylon.

A young man named Daniel and his three friends were captured too. They were very smart, so the king trained them in the ways of the Babylonians. Then he made them part of his special team of advisors. This team gave the king advice to help him run his country.

The king made a good choice! God gave Daniel and his friends great wisdom.

141

One night, the king had a bad
dream. He asked some of his advisors
what it meant.

"Tell us what you dreamed," the advisors said.

"No," said the king. "You tell me what I dreamed.
Then I'll be sure that you know what it means."

The advisors were afraid. "We can't do that. No one can!"

The king got angry and ordered his soldiers to kill all of
his advisors.

Daniel heard about the king's order. This meant he and his friends would die too. Daniel and his friends prayed, and God showed Daniel the king's dream. Daniel praised God and thanked him.

The next day, Daniel went to see King Nebuchadnezzar.

The king asked, "Can you tell me what I dreamed and what it meant?"

"No one on earth can do that," Daniel replied. "But there is a God who lives in heaven. He showed me what you dreamed, and he showed me what it means."

Daniel told the king about his dream. "You saw a huge statue of a man, made of gold, silver, and bronze. Its feet were made of iron and clay. A stone hit the feet, and the statue fell to pieces. Then the stone turned into a mountain that covered the whole world."

The king was amazed. That was exactly what he had dreamed!

Daniel said, "God is showing you what will happen in the future. The statue stands for four kingdoms. Yours is the first, and then there will be three more. Then a fifth one will come—God's kingdom! That's the stone in your dream. God's kingdom will put an end to all other kingdoms, but it will last forever."

The king stood from his throne and bowed down to Daniel. He believed what Daniel said. There really was a God in heaven! "Your God is greater than any other god," the king told Daniel. "He is greater than any king!"

MORE GEMS

Believe in God.
—Acts 16:34

He exists.
—Hebrews 11:6

Stand firm in your faith.

—Isaiah 7:9

Daniel's Friends Stand Tall for God

Daniel 3

King Nebuchadnezzar must have forgotten his dream. He must have forgotten that there really is a God in heaven. Because the king set up a giant gold statue outdoors and gave an order: "Everyone must bow down and worship this statue. Anyone who doesn't bow down will be thrown into a blazing furnace."

Daniel's three friends—Shadrach, Meshach, and Abednego—knew this was wrong. God had said, "I am the Lord. Worship me. Don't bow down and worship anything else." What were they going to do?

A large crowd was gathered in front of the statue. The king's musicians started playing their instruments, and all the people bowed to the ground.

Except Shadrach, Meshach, and Abednego!

They stood tall and firm, refusing to kneel.

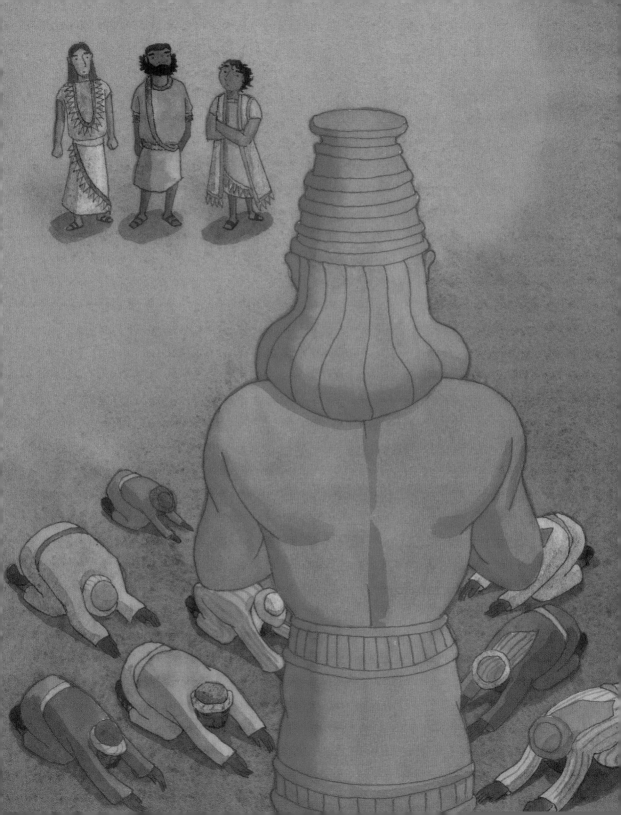

When the king heard about this, he was angry. He sent for the three young men and asked them, "Is it true that you disobeyed my order? You'd better bow down to the statue! If you don't, you'll be thrown into the furnace."

Meshach replied, "King Nebuchadnezzar, you can throw us into the furnace if you like. We know our God can save us. Even if he doesn't, we won't worship your statue."

Now the king was furious. "Make the furnace red-hot," he told his servants. "Make it seven times hotter than usual!" Then he ordered his soldiers to tie up the men's hands with rope. "Shove them into the flames!" he shouted.

The soldiers pushed the three men into the furnace. It was so hot that the soldiers were killed. But not Shadrach, Meshach, and Abednego. Even in the middle of the flames, they were still standing tall.

The king couldn't believe his eyes. "What's going on?" he asked his officials. "We threw three men into the furnace, but now I see four in there. And the fourth one is shining brightly."

Running to the furnace door, the king cried, "Shadrach, Meshach, and Abednego! Come out!"

The three young men walked out of the furnace. The fire hadn't touched them. They didn't even smell like smoke.

The only thing that had burned was the rope around their wrists. That was gone. Their hands were free.

King Nebuchadnezzar praised God for rescuing the three men. And he praised them for their rock-solid loyalty to God. "I'm giving a new order," the king said. "From now on, no one can say anything bad about your God. He is a mighty Savior!"

MORE GEMS

Stand your ground.
—Ephesians 6:13

Let nothing move you.
—1 Corinthians 15:58

The righteous stand firm forever.
—Proverbs 10:25

The Lord will rescue me.

—2 Timothy 4:18

God Saves Daniel from the Lions

Daniel 6

When King Darius took over Babylonia, he made Daniel one of his officials. Daniel did such a good job that King Darius decided to put him in charge of the whole kingdom. This upset the other officials, and they looked for a way to get rid of Daniel.

But Daniel was honest and did everything right. They couldn't find any reason for the king to be angry with him.

Then one of them had an idea. "Daniel prays to his God three times every day," he said. "Maybe we can use that to get him in trouble."

The officials went to King Darius and said, "You should make a law saying that anyone who prays to anybody but you will be thrown into the lions' den."

So the king wrote down this law and put his royal mark on it. The king liked this idea. He didn't know it was a trick to hurt Daniel.

Daniel knew the law was wrong. It went against God's rules. So he kept praying to the Lord, as he always did.

The officials told on him. "King Darius," they said, "Daniel is breaking the law! He must be punished."

The king wanted to save Daniel, but Daniel had broken the law. So the king ordered his soldiers to throw Daniel to the lions.

The soldiers shoved Daniel into the den, then pushed a large stone in front of the opening. Daniel heard King Darius shout, "You've been faithful to your God, Daniel. I hope he saves you!"

It was dark in the den, and Daniel could barely see the lions. Their eyes seemed to glow. The lions began pacing slowly around him, moving closer. One of them snarled, and Daniel saw its teeth.

Suddenly, a blazing light filled the den. Daniel shielded his eyes, then looked. A powerful angel stood beside him. The lions were cowering in the corner.

The next morning, King Darius rushed to see what happened. As his soldiers rolled away the stone, he peered into the den. "Daniel! Has your God kept you safe?"

Daniel replied, "Yes, King Darius! My God sent an angel to keep the lions away."

The king was so glad. Quickly, he told his soldiers to pull Daniel out. They all looked at Daniel. There wasn't a scratch on him. He had trusted in God, and God had protected him.

Then the king wrote a new law. He put his royal mark on it, and he sent it out to all the people in his kingdom. The new law said, "Everyone must honor Daniel's God. He is the one, true God. He performs miracles, and he reigns forever. This God rescues his people. He saved Daniel from the lions!"

MORE GEMS

God will save his people.
—Zechariah 9:16

He rescues and he saves.
—Daniel 6:27

Save me, LORD.
—Psalm 40:13

Overcome evil with good.

—Romans 12:21

Esther Stops an Evil Plan

Esther 1–10

King Xerxes ruled over the land of Persia. One day, the king got angry with his queen and sent her away. Now he needed another queen. So young women from all over Persia were brought to the city of Susa, where King Xerxes lived. He held a contest to see who should be the new queen.

The winner was a beautiful girl named Esther. The king liked her best.

Nobody was more surprised than Esther! That's because Esther wasn't a Persian. She was a Jew.

Esther had been raised by her cousin, Mordecai. He was a good man. When Esther became queen, he warned her, "Don't tell anyone you're a Jew." Some of the Persians hated Jews, and Mordecai wanted to protect her.

Esther had always obeyed Mordecai, so she kept the secret.

One day, a man named Haman walked past Mordecai. Haman was an important man in Persia. Everyone was supposed to honor him. But Mordecai wouldn't bow down.

That made Haman angry. He wanted Mordecai killed. And because Mordecai was a Jew, Haman wanted all the Jews killed.

So Haman told King Xerxes, "Jews are bad, and we have to get rid of them. You should order the Persians to kill them all." The king believed Haman and gave the order.

Mordecai sent a message to Esther: "Ask the king to save our people!"

Esther replied, "Anyone who goes to the king without being invited will be put to death—unless the king holds up his scepter when he sees them."

Mordecai said, "Maybe God made you queen so you can help us all."

Esther thought about this. Then she told Mordecai, "Tell our people to fast and pray for three days. I'll fast and pray too. Then I'll go to the king, even if it costs me my life."

Three days later, Esther put on her royal robe and went to the king's hall. The king was sitting on his throne. King Xerxes smiled and raised his scepter. Esther walked up to him, and he asked, "What do you want, Queen Esther? I'll do anything for you."

Esther told the king that Haman had tricked him. "He said you should order the Persians to kill all the Jews," she said. "But I'm a Jew. The Jews are my people. Please save our lives!"

King Xerxes was furious at Haman. The king gave a new order to protect the Jews and had Haman killed instead.

All the Jews in Persia were happy. They held a great celebration, because Esther and Mordecai had rescued their people. Faced with evil, they stood up for what was right. Esther had even risked her life. Together, Esther and Mordecai overcame evil with good.

MORE GEMS

Everyone born
of God
overcomes.

—1 John 5:4

We are more
than
conquerors.

—Romans 8:37

Fear no evil.

—Psalm 23:4

I am the Lord's servant.

—Luke 1:38

Mary and Joseph Follow God's Plan

Luke 1:26-38; Matthew 1:18-25; Luke 2:1-7

God sent an angel to a young woman named Mary. The angel told her, "God is pleased with you, Mary. He has chosen you to do something very special for him. You're going to have a baby. God wants you to name him Jesus. He will be God's Son, and he'll set up a kingdom that will last forever."

At first, Mary was scared. Then she was puzzled. How could this be true? She wasn't married yet! But Mary loved God and wanted to obey him. So she told the angel, "I am the Lord's servant. I'll do what he wants me to do."

God also sent an angel to Joseph, who was engaged to Mary. Joseph was sleeping. In his dream, the angel told him, "The baby that Mary will have is from God. So it's okay for you to make Mary your wife. Name the baby Jesus. He will save people from their sins."

Like Mary, Joseph was God's servant. He loved God and wanted to obey him. So Joseph decided to do what God had told him to do.

A few months passed, and Mary was going to have the baby soon. Then one day, the emperor of Rome gave an order. He wanted to know how many people lived in his empire. So everyone had to go to his or her hometown to be counted.

"We have to go to Bethlehem," Joseph told Mary. "My family is from that town."

They had to obey the emperor's order.

The trip to Bethlehem was rough. Joseph walked, leading the donkey that Mary rode. When they reached Bethlehem, Joseph and Mary were tired. But there was no place to stay. Many people had come to be counted, and all the guest rooms were full.

Joseph was worried. It was time for the baby to be born!

Finally, he found a spot—a stable filled with animals. It would have to do. At least there was some straw for Mary to lie on.

Then the baby came. And in that cold, smelly stable, Mary and Joseph saw little Jesus for the first time. They were so glad they had chosen to serve the Lord. God's plan for their lives was part of his bigger plan to bless the world. God had used them to bring everyone a Savior!

MORE GEMS

Serve the LORD.
—Joshua 24:15

Serve him faithfully.
—1 Samuel 12:24

A Savior has been born.

—Luke 2:11

Shepherds Hear the Good News

Luke 2:8-20

In a field near Bethlehem, some shepherds were watching their sheep. One shepherd looked up at the stars. *It's so peaceful here*, he thought.

Suddenly, he saw a brilliant light. A dazzling angel appeared.

The shepherd fell down, dropping his staff. He lay with his arms over his head.

"Don't be afraid," the angel said. "I have good news for the whole world! It will bring everyone so much joy."

The shepherd opened his eyes. His friends were lying on the ground, looking scared. He wondered what the angel's news could be.

The angel pointed at the town. "Today in Bethlehem, a Savior has been born. He's the Messiah, God's chosen one. And he is the Lord, the ruler of all the earth. He's the one everybody is waiting for. Look for a little baby, lying in a manger, wrapped in cloths. He is the Savior of the world!"

All at once, angels filled the sky. They were praising God, singing,

"Glory to God!
And peace on earth.
Peace and joy to everyone
who has God's blessing."

Then the angels were gone.

The shepherd and his friends looked at each other. Picking up his staff, the shepherd said, "Let's go see!"

He and his friends left the sheep and hurried to Bethlehem. They looked for stables because that was the best place to find a manger.

Most of the stables were dark. But in one, a light glowed. Hearing soft voices, the shepherds peered inside. There, with the donkeys, goats, and sheep, was a man and a woman. They were kneeling next to something on the floor.

The shepherd stepped forward. His friends pressed in behind him.

Looking up, the man and woman smiled. And the shepherd saw what lay between them. There in a manger, wrapped in cloths, was a tiny baby boy. Just as the angel said.

Gazing at the baby, the shepherd believed the angel's words. He knew this child had come to save the world. The shepherd's heart filled with hope and joy.

He grabbed his friends. "We can't keep this to ourselves. We have to tell others!"

The shepherd and his friends ran through the streets, calling to everyone they saw. The people were amazed at the men's story, and hope stirred in their hearts too.

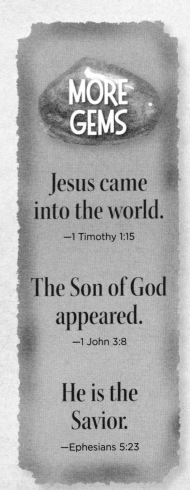

MORE GEMS

Jesus came into the world.
—1 Timothy 1:15

The Son of God appeared.
—1 John 3:8

He is the Savior.
—Ephesians 5:23

Seek the LORD.

—Deuteronomy 4:29

The Magi Search for Jesus

Matthew 2:1-12

God told the Jews about Jesus's birth by sending angels to some shepherds. He told other people in the world by sending a star to some scientists.

These scientists were known as magi, or wise men. They studied the sky, watching the sun and the moon, the stars and the planets. So God put a sign in the sky to lead them to Jesus. It was a clue they couldn't miss.

"Look at this!" said one of the magi. "There's a new star in the sky tonight."

They studied the writing on their scrolls to discover what the new star meant.

"A new king has been born—the king of the Jews!"

"He must be very important."

"Let's follow the star and go see him."

The magi loaded up their camels. They packed tents, clothes, food, and water. And they brought gold, frankincense, and myrrh. Gold was beautiful and valuable. Frankincense smelled good when it was burned. And myrrh was a strong, tart spice. Perfect gifts for a special king!

After a long journey, the magi reached Jerusalem. They asked, "Where is the new king? We've come to worship him."

King Herod heard about the magi and what they were looking for. He knew that someday a Savior would come to be Israel's new king. Herod asked his advisors where the Messiah was supposed to be born. "In Bethlehem," they answered.

So King Herod met with the magi in secret. "Go to Bethlehem and search for this child," he told them. "When you find him, tell me where he is. I want to go worship him too."

The magi left Jerusalem and headed to Bethlehem. One of them pointed at the sky. "Look! The star is still leading us."

The star went ahead of them, guiding them to the small town. Then it stopped over one of the houses.

Inside, they found Mary and Jesus. The magi were overjoyed. They had come so far, seeking the Lord, and now they had found him. Bowing, they worshiped Jesus. Then one by one, they offered him their gifts.

That night, in a dream, an angel told them not to say anything to King Herod. That man didn't want to worship Jesus— he wanted to get rid of him. So the next morning, the magi got on their camels and traveled home, taking a different path, away from Jerusalem.

MORE GEMS

Seek the Lord and live.
—Amos 5:6

You will find him.
—Deuteronomy 4:29

Honor your father and mother.

—Ephesians 6:2

Jesus Surprises Everyone

Luke 2:41–52

Every year, Jesus's family went to Jerusalem to celebrate a holiday called Passover. There was a festival in the city, and Jews came from all over the world. Everyone visited the temple to worship God, and families ate a special meal together.

When Jesus was twelve years old, he and his family got ready to go to the festival. Mary told Jesus, "Please get me another basket, so I can finish packing the food for our journey."

"Yes, Mother," Jesus said, and he promptly obeyed. Soon all the preparations were done, and the family left for Jerusalem.

The trip took a few days. Aunts and uncles and cousins came along, and friends of Jesus's family came too. Sometimes Jesus walked with his mother and father, and sometimes he walked with his other relatives.

The festival was exciting. Jesus loved seeing all the people in the city. He loved going to the temple. And the food tasted great!

The next morning, the group headed home. Everyone was talking and laughing as they walked along the road. Jesus wasn't with his parents, but that was okay. They thought he was having fun with his cousins. That evening, the group set up camp, and everyone got ready for bed.

Joseph tied the last rope on the tent. Then he asked Mary, "Have you seen Jesus?"

"I'm sure he'll be here soon," she said, laying out their mats.

But Jesus didn't show up. Joseph and Mary looked around and asked if anyone had seen him. Nobody knew where he was!

That night, Joseph and Mary were too worried to sleep. When the sun rose, they went back to Jerusalem to search for Jesus.

They looked all over the city. After three days, they finally found him.

Jesus was in the courtyard of the temple. He was sitting there listening to the teachers, asking them questions and answering theirs. Everyone was amazed at what Jesus said. He was so wise!

Mary said, "Son, why did you leave us? We were very worried!"

Respectfully, Jesus said, "I had to be here, in my Father's house. Didn't you know that?"

Mary looked at Joseph. They were relieved and happy to find Jesus. They told him it was time to go home. Jesus obeyed and said goodbye to the teachers at the temple.

After that, Jesus went home with his parents. He was a good son, who always honored his father and mother and listened to them. This pleased God, his Father in heaven.

MORE GEMS

Children, obey your parents.
—Ephesians 6:1

Obey your parents in everything.
—Colossians 3:20

Show proper respect to everyone.
—1 Peter 2:17

Resist the devil.

—James 4:7

Jesus Battles Satan

Matthew 3:13–4:11; Mark 1:9–13; Luke 3:21–4:13

When Jesus grew up, his cousin John baptized him in the Jordan River. The Holy Spirit came down from heaven onto Jesus, like a dove landing on his shoulder. And everyone heard God say, "This is my Son. I love him, and I'm very pleased with him!"

It was time for Jesus to start doing what God sent him to do—teach people about God's kingdom, heal their sicknesses, and set them free from sin. Jesus was almost ready, but first he had to do one more thing.

The Holy Spirit led Jesus into the desert, to face God's enemy, Satan, who is also called the devil.

In the desert, Jesus and Satan fought a big battle. But not with their hands or with weapons. Satan attacked with temptations and lies. Jesus fought back with prayer and God's words.

The battle lasted forty days. During that time, Jesus fasted, which means he didn't eat anything. Instead of eating, he prayed. When Satan attacked, Jesus's body was weak. But his spirit was strong.

"You must be hungry," the devil said. He looked around. There was no food anywhere. "Aren't you God's Son? Turn some rocks into bread so you can eat!"

Jesus shook his head. He was hungry, but he wasn't fooled. "God said people need more than bread to live—they need every word he says."

Satan tried another trick. He took Jesus to the top of God's temple. Then he said, "If you really are the Son of God, prove it. Jump! God said his angels will protect you."

Again Jesus refused. "God also said people must never test him like that."

Taking Jesus to the top of a mountain, the devil tried one more time. He showed Jesus the kingdoms of the world. They glittered with silver and gold. "They're all mine, but you can have them," Satan said. "Just bow down and worship me."

But Jesus said no. "God said people must worship him only," he told Satan. "Now go away!"

MORE GEMS

Stand against
the devil's
schemes.
—Ephesians 6:11

Overcome
the evil one.
—1 John 2:14

Then the devil left, and angels brought food to Jesus and took care of him.

Jesus resisted Satan and won. Now people know how to resist the devil too!

Follow Christ.

—1 Corinthians 1:12

Jesus Invites Some Fishermen to Join Him

Luke 5:1-11

One day Jesus went to the seashore. As he talked to the fishermen, a crowd gathered. Everyone was trying to get close to him.

Seeing an empty boat nearby, Jesus stepped into it. He said to the owner, Simon, "Please take me out into the water." Simon and his partners gave the boat a push and hopped in. Then Simon turned the boat so Jesus could speak to the people back on shore.

Jesus taught about God's kingdom. Everyone was amazed at the things he said.

When he was done, Jesus told Simon, "Take us out to deeper water, and throw out your nets. Let's catch some fish!"

Simon said, "We've been working all night, and we haven't caught a thing." Jesus just smiled. So Simon shrugged. "Okay, if you say so. We'll try again."

They went farther out
to sea, and the fishermen
tossed their nets. "This is a
waste of time," Simon whispered
to his brother, Andrew. Nodding,
Andrew said, "I know!" Then they
started hauling in the nets.

Simon's rope was hard to pull, and he felt
something wiggling at the end of it. Surprised,
he tugged harder. All the men pulled as hard as they
could. The water began splashing and foaming. Then the
nets came up, filled with fish!

The nets were so full that they started to break. Simon
called to some fishermen in another boat. "James! John!
Come help us!" They brought their boat next to Simon's. All
the men worked together to bring the catch into the boats.
There were so many fish! Simon couldn't believe what was
happening.

He looked at Jesus. Jesus was just sitting there
grinning. Something stirred in Simon's heart.
He could tell Jesus was someone special.
That scared Simon a little, because
Simon knew he was a sinful
person, just like everyone else.

Jesus said, "Don't be afraid, Simon. Just follow me. I want you to be my disciple. I'm going to teach you how to catch something better than fish. I'm going to show you how to fish for people!"

Finally, the boats reached the shore. Again, Jesus asked Simon to come with him. He also asked Andrew, James, and John to follow him. The four men looked at everything they had— the boats, the nets, and all the fish they had just caught. Then they left it all behind and followed Jesus.

Come near to God.

—James 4:8

Zacchaeus Climbs a Tree

Luke 19:1–10

The people in Jericho were excited.

"What's happening?" a man asked a woman. She was hurrying toward the city gate with everyone else.

"Jesus is coming!" she said.

"Here, to our town?"

"Yes, right here!"

Zacchaeus was excited too. Normally, he didn't get too excited. He was a tax collector, and he spent most of his time counting money. He had grown rich by cheating people, making them pay more taxes than they owed.

People like Zacchaeus don't usually go running down the street. But today he was running. He had heard amazing things about Jesus, and he wanted to see him.

There was just one problem. A crowd had gathered, and Zacchaeus wasn't very tall. He couldn't see anything.

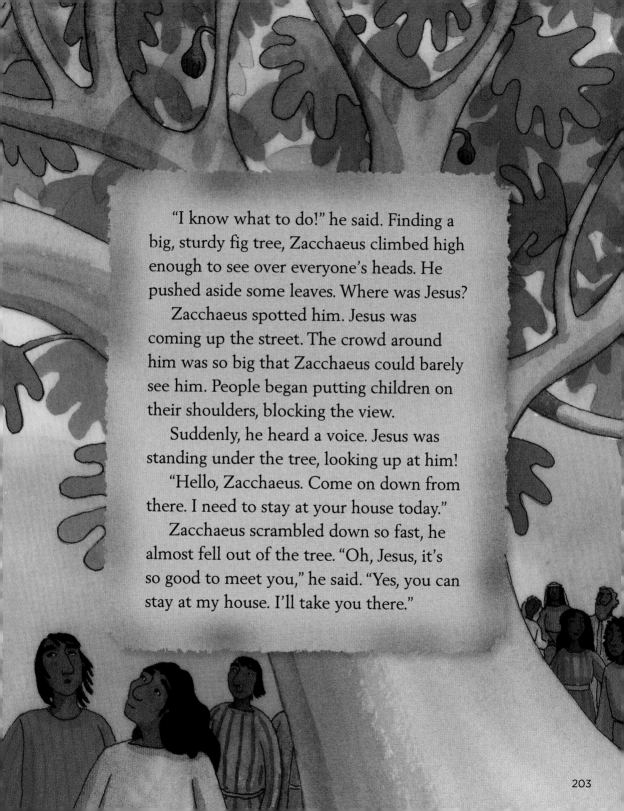

"I know what to do!" he said. Finding a big, sturdy fig tree, Zacchaeus climbed high enough to see over everyone's heads. He pushed aside some leaves. Where was Jesus?

Zacchaeus spotted him. Jesus was coming up the street. The crowd around him was so big that Zacchaeus could barely see him. People began putting children on their shoulders, blocking the view.

Suddenly, he heard a voice. Jesus was standing under the tree, looking up at him!

"Hello, Zacchaeus. Come on down from there. I need to stay at your house today."

Zacchaeus scrambled down so fast, he almost fell out of the tree. "Oh, Jesus, it's so good to meet you," he said. "Yes, you can stay at my house. I'll take you there."

MORE GEMS

Approach
God.
—Ephesians 3:12

"Come to me."
—Matthew 11:28

Smiling, Zacchaeus led Jesus to his home. They sat at the table, and Jesus told him about God's kingdom and about sin and forgiveness. Zacchaeus was so glad to hear all this, he promised to give half of his riches to the poor. He also promised to pay back everyone he had cheated. He was going to be honest from now on!

That day, Zacchaeus met God (because Jesus is God). And Zacchaeus learned something wonderful: If you draw near to God, he will draw near to you. Jesus loves you just the way you are. He will forgive your sins and help you become the person you were meant to be.

Do not worry.

—Matthew 6:25

Martha Tries to Be a Good Host

Luke 10:38–42

Jesus and his disciples visited a village called Bethany. It was on the side of a mountain near Jerusalem. There they met a woman named Martha. "Please, come to my home," she said. "Stay with my brother and sister and me. We have plenty of food to share."

"Thank you," Jesus said. "We'll be happy to stay with you." So she led them to her house.

Martha was excited that Jesus and his disciples had come for a visit. When they entered her home, she realized there was so much to do! She needed to cook a big meal. She had to set the table. And she had to find enough mats for everyone to sleep on. Taking a deep breath, she thought, *at least my brother and sister can help*.

Martha worked hard to get things ready. As she reached for flour, she called for her brother. "Lazarus! Can you start the fire so I can bake some bread?" But he didn't answer.

Taking a pitcher, she poured water for Jesus and his friends. Her sister, Mary, was sitting on the floor next to Jesus. Martha motioned for Mary to get up and help. But Mary didn't see her. She was listening to Jesus.

Martha didn't know how she was going to get everything done. She muttered to herself as she kneaded the dough. "I shouldn't have to do all this alone. Mary and Lazarus should be working too! How can I take good care of my guests if I don't have any help?" She was getting very worried now.

She went to see if Jesus needed anything. Mary was still sitting there. Martha couldn't take it anymore. She complained to Jesus. "There's so much to do, and Mary isn't helping a bit. She's letting me do all the work. Don't you see that? Please tell her to help me!"

Jesus put a hand on her arm. "Martha, listen. You're worried and upset about so many things. Don't be! The meal doesn't have to be perfect. We'll get enough to eat. And we don't have to be perfectly comfortable. We'll sleep fine. Only one thing in life really matters, and Mary has chosen that. It is seeking God's kingdom by spending time with me. Instead of pulling her away from me, why don't you join her?"

Smiling, Jesus added, "Don't worry, Martha. If you focus on God's kingdom first, he'll take care of all the rest."

MORE GEMS

Do not be anxious.
—Philippians 4:6

Seek first his kingdom.
—Matthew 6:33

God loves a cheerful giver.

—2 Corinthians 9:7

A Poor Woman Gives a Big Gift

Mark 12:41–44; Luke 21:1–4

Jesus and his disciples were at the temple one day. He sat down and watched people make offerings to God. Lots of men and women came, bringing money to give God as a gift. This was one way the Israelites worshiped God.

Many of them were rich, and they carried large bags of money. Walking up to the box, they opened their bags and poured in gold and silver coins. Some made sure people were watching. They held up their bags and shook them. Then they slowly poured in their coins so their gift would look bigger.

Then a woman came along. She didn't have a big bag of money. She didn't have a bag at all. Jesus knew she was poor. Her husband had died, and she didn't have anyone to take care of her. But the woman didn't seem sad. She was smiling.

Jesus could see that her heart was full of love for God. She had come to worship God and thank him for his blessings. She was happy to bring her gift to him.

"Watch this," Jesus told his disciples. They all turned to see the woman.

She went to the box, held out her hand, and dropped in two tiny copper coins. The woman wasn't dressed in fancy clothes. And the two coins weren't worth much. No one had been impressed by her gift.

Except Jesus.

The woman pulled her cloak around her and left the temple. As she walked past Jesus and the disciples, her face was beaming with joy.

"Did you see that?" Jesus said. "All those other people put in lots of money. She gave just two small coins. But they're rich, and she isn't. They gave just a little of their money, and she gave all she had. Do you understand what just happened? This woman gave God the biggest gift of all."

MORE GEMS

The righteous
give
generously.
—Psalm 37:21

Freely give.
—Matthew 10:8

The LORD is my shepherd.

—Psalm 23:1

Jesus Describes God's Love for All People

Psalm 23; Isaiah 40:11; Luke 15:1-7; John 10:1-18

Some people got upset with Jesus because he spent time with sinners. He talked to sinners. He visited their homes. He even ate meals with sinners. That seemed wrong. Wasn't God angry with people who broke his rules? Didn't he want to punish them?

So Jesus told a story.

In Jesus's story, a shepherd was watching over his flock one evening. He was a good shepherd who cared deeply for his sheep. He fed them, guided them, and protected them.

"The sun is going down," the shepherd said, looking at the sky. "It's time to take the sheep back to their pen."

Before the shepherd led his sheep home, he wanted to make sure they were all there. So he walked through the field, counting them. He came to the last three sheep.

"… ninety-seven, ninety-eight, ninety-nine."

The shepherd scratched his head. "That's not right," he said. "There should be one hundred." He counted his sheep again. Only ninety-nine.

"One is missing!" he said. He looked around at the hills near the field. The sheep was nowhere in sight.

He looked at the others. They were happily munching grass. "They'll be safe here while I go after the lost one," he said. Then he hurried off to find the missing sheep.

The shepherd searched all over. He climbed up into the hills and down into the gullies. He looked behind large rocks and inside dark caves. All the time, he kept calling for the lost sheep.

Then the shepherd heard a noise. It was his sheep bleating. The sheep was answering his voice!

Following the sound, he found the missing sheep. It had fallen into a big hole. "There you are," he said. "I've been looking everywhere for you."

The shepherd jumped into the hole. He petted the sheep, made sure it wasn't hurt, and helped it climb out. Then he carried it back on his shoulders.

When he brought the flock home, the shepherd told his friends, "Let's celebrate! I found my lost sheep!"

Jesus's story ended there. He said, "That's the way God feels about sinners. He loves everyone. When someone wanders away from him, God goes looking for them. He calls out to them, and when they respond to him, he rescues them. He is very glad when that person is back with him, and all the angels in heaven cheer!"

MORE GEMS

The Lord watches over you.
—Psalm 121:5

"I am the good shepherd."
—John 10:11

Love your neighbor.

—Luke 10:27

A Man Helps a Stranger

Luke 10:25-37

One day, Jesus was teaching a crowd of people. A man asked him, "What do I have to do if I want to live forever?"

"What do God's rules say?" Jesus replied.

The man thought for a moment. "First, I need to love God with all my heart. Second, I need to love my neighbor as much as I love myself."

Jesus smiled. The man knew God's rules well. He had just said the two most important ones! "That's right," Jesus told him. "If you do those things, you'll live with God in heaven forever."

"But who is my neighbor?" the man asked.

"Here, let me explain," Jesus said.

A man was walking down a road. The man was a Jew, and he was going from Jerusalem to another city. Some thieves attacked him, took everything he had, beat him up, and left him next to the road. The man was badly hurt. He couldn't get up or cry for help.

Soon a priest came along. He was a Jew, just like the man beside the road. The priest saw the man lying there. But instead of helping him, he kept walking.

Then a Levite came down the road. He was also a Jew. He spotted the man, but he didn't stop to help either.

Then along came a Samaritan, leading a donkey. Samaritans and Jews didn't like each other. Yet when the Samaritan saw the man, he went to him. He knew the man needed help.

The Samaritan gently wrapped up the man's wounds and put him on his donkey. Then he took the man to an inn. There he cared for the man for the rest of the day and all that night. He gave him water when he was thirsty and food when he was hungry.

In the morning, the Samaritan had to leave. Handing the innkeeper some money, he said, "Please look after this man. I'll come back soon. If you spend more money than this, I'll pay you back." The Samaritan said goodbye to the man and wished him well.

Jesus looked at the man who had asked him the questions. "So, what do you think? Who acted like a neighbor to the wounded man?"

"The one who stopped to help him," the man replied.

Jesus nodded. "That's right. And you should act the same way."

Return to the LORD.

—Joel 2:13

A Wayward Son Goes Home

Luke 15:11–32

A young Jewish man grew up in a nice home and enjoyed a good life. The young man's father had lots of land and animals and servants. His father also loved him and treated him well.

The young man had to help out on the farm, planting seeds, harvesting crops, and feeding the cows and sheep. But he didn't like working so hard. So he told his father, "I know that when you die, I will get a part of everything you own. I don't want to wait. Give me my share of the money today, so I can go live the way I want to live."

The father's feelings were hurt. He knew his son was making a big mistake. But the father gave the son what he wanted and let him leave.

The young man moved to a faraway country. For a while, he had a great time. He made lots of friends because he bought food and gifts for people. Everyone around him had fun.

But soon he had spent all his money. His friends went away, and he started to go hungry. So he asked a farmer for a job feeding the pigs. It was dirty, smelly work. As the young man filled the troughs, his stomach growled. The pigs had lots to munch on, but he had nothing.

The young man remembered his father's servants. *Their lives are better than mine*, he thought. *They work hard, but they have plenty to eat.*

He knew he had sinned. So he did the best thing any sinner can do—he decided to repent. He would admit he made a mistake and choose to do right. So the young man went home.

His father saw him coming and ran to him. He gave his son a big hug!

The young man was surprised. "I sinned, Father," he said. "I'm not good enough to be your son anymore."

He asked his father to make him a servant. But his father wasn't listening. He was talking to the servants. "Dress him in my best robe, get him some sandals, and put a gold ring on his finger. Then prepare a big meal, and let's celebrate! My son was gone, and now he's back."

The young man started obeying his father again. He was part of the family once more. And he always had good things to eat. The father had forgiven the young man, just as God forgives anyone who repents and returns to him.

MORE GEMS

Repent and
turn to God.
—Acts 26:20

Be earnest
and repent.
—Revelation 3:19

Be reconciled
to God.
—2 Corinthians 5:20

Don't be afraid; just believe.

—Mark 5:36

Jesus Saves a Young Girl

Mark 5:21–43

A man named Jairus was hurrying to the seashore. People greeted him on the street, but he rushed past without a reply. His mission was too important.

Finally, he reached the Sea of Galilee. On the shore, a crowd had gathered to see Jesus.

Jairus pushed his way through the people and fell at Jesus's feet. "Please come to my home," he begged. "My little girl is very sick. I'm afraid she's going to die! Please come and heal her."

Putting a hand on his shoulder, Jesus said, "Of course I'll come."

The crowd followed them. Before they reached Jairus's house,
some people came out and stopped them. "We're so sorry," the
people told Jairus. "Your daughter is dead. It won't do any good for
Jesus to come now."

Dropping to his knees, Jairus began to cry. But Jesus told him,
"Don't be afraid; just believe."

Jairus wiped his eyes, got up, and led Jesus to his home. Jesus told three of his disciples—Simon, James, and John—to come with them. Everyone else stayed behind.

At the house, people were crying and wailing. Everyone was so sad because the girl had died. All their hope was gone.

But Jesus knew something they didn't—he could do miracles!

Jairus and his wife led Jesus and the three disciples to the girl. She was not moving or breathing. Jesus took her hand and told her to get up.

Holding his wife close, Jairus watched. Suddenly, his little girl sat up. Jairus was amazed. He and his wife ran to their daughter and hugged her.

Jesus smiled. "Maybe you should get her some food," he said. "She might need something to eat."

The girl turned to him and nodded. "I am a little hungry."

Everyone laughed, and Jairus rushed out of the room. Now he had a new mission!

MORE GEMS

Jesus Christ heals you.
—Acts 9:34

Put your hope in God.
—Psalm 42:5

Trust in the LORD forever.
—Isaiah 26:4

Jesus is the Messiah.

—John 20:31

Simon Says Who Jesus Is

Matthew 16:13–20

Jesus visited many towns. He spoke to people in synagogues, the places where the Jewish people worship God. He also spoke to big crowds outdoors, on a mountain or at the seashore. He taught about God, and he healed people who were sick.

Most people didn't understand who Jesus was. They knew his name, but they didn't know what made him so special. Was he a teacher? Was he a doctor? "Isn't this the son of Joseph, the carpenter?" one man asked his wife. "Isn't Jesus a carpenter too? How does he know so much?"

One day, Jesus and his disciples arrived at a place he wanted to visit. Before a crowd gathered, Jesus asked the disciples a question.

"Who do the people think I am?"

The disciples looked at each other. Finally, Andrew shrugged. "Well, some people say you're John the Baptist." He felt a little silly saying it, but some people really thought that. John the Baptist had died. And people were saying that Jesus was John raised from the dead.

James cleared his throat. "Some people say you're Elijah." That seemed kind of silly too. Elijah was a prophet who had lived long ago. But some people believed he had come back as Jesus.

Philip raised his hand a little. "Some people think you're Jeremiah or some other prophet from the past." He put his hand down. That idea sounded just as foolish as the others.

Jesus looked around at his disciples. "What about all of you?" he asked. "Who do you believe I am?"

Simon answered right away. "You're the Messiah, the leader God promised to send to save his people. You're God's Son!"

Smiling, Jesus put his hand on Simon's shoulder. "You are blessed, Simon," he said. "No human being told you this. My Father showed it to you. And now I'm naming you Peter, which means rock. That's because the truth that I'm the Messiah is rock-solid. Since you believe it, you too are solid as a rock."

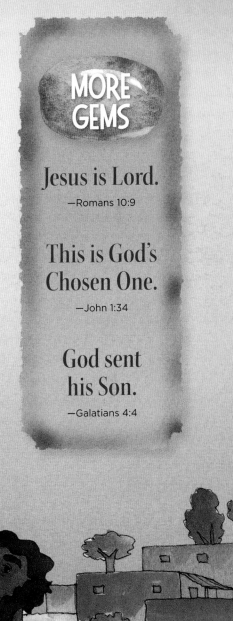

MORE GEMS

Jesus is Lord.
—Romans 10:9

This is God's Chosen One.
—John 1:34

God sent his Son.
—Galatians 4:4

Let your light shine.

—Matthew 5:16

Jesus Shows His Glory

Matthew 5:14–16; 17:1–13; Mark 9:2–13; John 8:12

One day, Jesus went up a tall mountain. He took along three of his disciples—Peter, James, and John. Jesus wanted to show them something wonderful. It would help them understand that he was God's Son.

At the top of the mountain, the disciples looked around. It was a
clear day with a blue sky. Suddenly, Peter, James, and John saw Jesus
shining like the sun!

His face was glowing brightly. His clothes were sparkling white.
Light was blazing all around him.

"What's happening?" James asked.

Peter was stunned. He closed his eyes, then opened them again.
Now it wasn't just Jesus standing there. Two men were standing
beside him—Moses and Elijah! *How can that be?* Peter thought. *They
lived a long, long time ago!*

The disciples were astonished. James and John just stood there, staring at Jesus. Peter thought he should say something. "Lord, it's … uh, it's good that we're all here," he stammered. "Do you want me to build some shelters?" He was so confused, he didn't know what else to say.

All at once, a bright cloud covered everything. It was sparkling with the same kind of light that was blazing from Jesus. Then the disciples heard God's voice!

"This is my Son, and I love him," God said. "Listen to what he says."

The disciples fell down. Peter covered his head with his arms. But a moment later he felt a touch on his shoulder. Jesus was leaning over him, smiling. Moses and Elijah were gone.

"It's okay. Don't be afraid," Jesus said. He took Peter's hand and pulled him to his feet. Then he helped up James and John too.

The three disciples didn't say a word as they walked down the mountain. Peter was thinking about what just happened. Jesus had shone with the glory of God! Peter knew that Jesus was God's Son.

Then Peter recalled something Jesus had taught them. Jesus had said, "I am the light of the world. And because you believe in me, you are the light of the world too. Let your light shine."

MORE GEMS

Live as children of light.
—Ephesians 5:8

Walk in the light.
—1 John 1:7

The righteous will shine.
—Matthew 13:43

Serve one another.

—Galatians 5:13

Jesus Washes Dirty Feet

John 13:1–17

Jesus wanted to show his disciples how much he loved them. He also wanted to show them how to love each other. So he decided to teach his disciples an important lesson.

One evening he did something strange to get their attention. They were all gathered in a room for a special meal.

During the meal, Jesus stood up, poured some water into a bowl, and picked up a towel. Then, without saying anything, he knelt on the floor and started washing the disciples' feet.

They were shocked. Jesus was acting like a servant! But he was the Son of God. He was the Messiah. He was too important to do something like this. Wasn't he?

Jesus just smiled. He knew who he was. But he kept washing their dirty, dusty feet.

He dried Matthew's toes with the towel, then moved over to Peter.

"Wait, Lord," Peter said. "Are you really going to wash my feet? No, no. It doesn't seem right."

Jesus looked up at him. "If I don't do this, you can't be my disciple."

Peter replied, "Then wash my whole body!"

"You've already had a bath," Jesus said, putting Peter's foot in the bowl. "You just need to have your feet washed. Then you'll be clean."

When Jesus had finished with everyone, he went back to his place at the table. All the disciples were amazed at what he had done!

"Do you understand what just happened?" Jesus asked. "You call me your teacher and your master. You're right—that's what I am. A teacher is greater than his students, and a master is greater than his servants. Yet I just washed your feet! I just served you, because I love you. I helped you by taking care of you. Now you've seen what it really means to be great. Take care of each other the same way. You'll be blessed if you do."

Christ died for our sins.

—1 Corinthians 15:3

Jesus Saves the World

Matthew 26–27; Mark 14–15; Luke 22–23; John 18–19

Jesus came to earth for many reasons. But most important, Jesus came to rescue people from their sins. To do this, Jesus was going to die on a cross to pay the penalty for everyone's sins. This was God's plan all along.

Jesus and his disciples were eating together for the last time before Jesus finished his mission on earth. In the middle of the meal, Judas got up from the table and left. The other disciples didn't know where he was going or why. But Jesus knew. Judas had made up his mind to betray Jesus. He was going to show the Jewish leaders who didn't like Jesus where they could find him and arrest him.

After the meal, Jesus led the other disciples to a garden, on the mountain near Jerusalem. Jesus knew he was going to die soon. He said, "Wait here while I go over there and pray."

Jesus had just finished praying when Judas walked into the garden. Behind him were soldiers and people carrying torches, clubs, and swords. "Hello, Teacher," said Judas, and he kissed Jesus on the cheek. That was Judas's signal to let the soldiers know which person was Jesus. The soldiers arrested Jesus and tied him up. Seeing this, the disciples got scared and ran away.

The soldiers took Jesus to the palace of the high priest. There the Jewish leaders put Jesus on trial. They found him guilty because he said he was God's Son, and to them that was a terrible lie. So they took Jesus to the Roman governor and said, "This man must be crucified!"

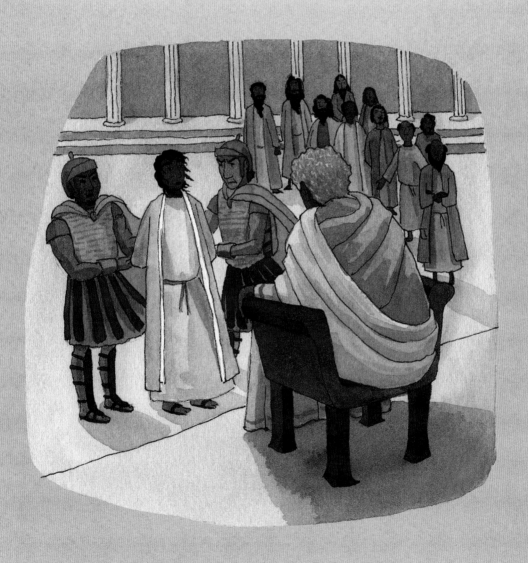

A crowd of Jewish people shouted, "Crucify him! Crucify him!" So the governor ordered his soldiers to do it.

The Roman soldiers made Jesus carry a heavy wooden cross to the top of a hill. Then they nailed Jesus to the cross. It hurt Jesus to die that way. But he loved people very much, and he did it so God would forgive them for their sins.

After suffering for six hours on the cross, Jesus said, "It is finished." Then he died. Jesus had done what God sent him to do. He had fulfilled God's plan to pay the price for all our sins. It was a sad day, but Jesus had given us a wonderful gift.

MORE GEMS

In Christ God forgave you.
Ephesians 4:32

Christ has set us free.
Galatians 5:1

My redeemer lives.

—Job 19:25

Jesus Comes Back to Life

Matthew 27:55–28:10; Mark 15:40–16:14; Luke 8:1–3; 23:47–24:12; John 19:25–20:18

When Jesus died on the cross, many people were there.

Mary Magdalene was one of them. She loved Jesus very much, and she wept as he died. The other women with her wept too.

Later, as the sun was going down, two men came to the cross. It was Joseph and Nicodemus. They believed in Jesus, and they wanted to make sure he was buried properly.

Mary watched the two men gently lower Jesus from the cross. They wrapped his body in a white cloth and then carried him to a nearby garden. Mary and the other women followed.

Joseph and Nicodemus put Jesus's body into a tomb carved in a hillside. The men rolled a big stone in front of the opening. Mary and the others stayed there at the tomb as long as they could. But when it got dark, they left the garden.

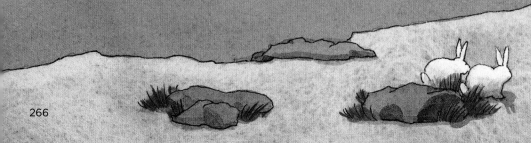

On Sunday morning, Mary and the other women went back to the tomb. Mary was sad. She thought, *Jesus was the Savior, the Redeemer! He was going to rescue us all from our sins. But he's dead. How can he save anyone now?*

When they entered the garden, one of the women pointed toward the tomb. "The stone has been moved!"

Mary and the others hurried over. The tomb was empty.

"His body is gone!" Mary gasped. Leaning on the big stone, she put her face in her hands and cried.

Suddenly, a bright light blazed out of the tomb. Mary looked inside. Two angels, shining brightly, were sitting where Jesus had been!

"Why are you weeping?" one of the angels asked.

In a trembling voice, Mary said, "Someone took Jesus's body."

Just then, Mary saw a man standing outside the tomb. She thought he was the gardener. "Did you take Jesus away?" she asked. "Please tell me where you put him!"

Holding out his hands, the man said one word: "Mary."

Instantly, she recognized his voice and knew he was Jesus. It was the sweetest sound Mary ever heard.

"Teacher!" she cried. Falling to the ground, she grasped his feet and worshiped him.

"Don't hold on to me now," he said. "Tell my disciples I'm going back to heaven. But before I do, I'll come see them."

Mary ran to find the disciples. Out of breath, she told them, "I saw Jesus! He's alive! Our Savior is alive!"

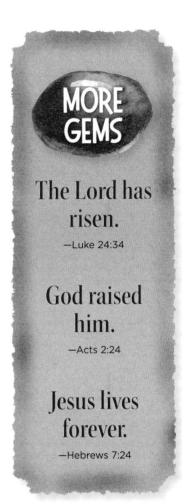

MORE GEMS

The Lord has risen.
—Luke 24:34

God raised him.
—Acts 2:24

Jesus lives forever.
—Hebrews 7:24

Go and make disciples.

—Matthew 28:19

Jesus Gives His Disciples a Mission

Matthew 28:16–20; Mark 16:9–20; Luke 24:13–53; John 20:19–21:25; Acts 1:1–11

The disciples were all hiding in a room with the door locked, afraid that the Jewish leaders might arrest them. Just like they had arrested Jesus. When the disciples heard Jesus was alive, they didn't believe it.

Mary tried to convince them she was speaking the truth. "I know he was crucified—I watched him die," she said. "But I'm telling you, he's alive!"

"How can that be?" Philip asked.

Nathanael shook his head. "He died on the cross. He can't be alive."

Later that day, there was a knock on the door. "Open up. It's me—Peter!"

James opened the door, and Peter rushed inside. "Listen, everyone!" he said. "Jesus is alive! I saw him with my own eyes. I was walking alone, and suddenly there he was. He started talking to me. It was really him!"

Mary nodded. The other disciples didn't know what to think.

That evening, as the disciples were eating dinner, Jesus appeared!
Smiling, he said, "Peace to all of you."

The disciples were shocked. Were they seeing a ghost? How did
Jesus get in?

Jesus held out his hands. "Don't be afraid. It's me! See my hands
and feet? You can touch me. I'm not a ghost."

The disciples crowded around him. This was amazing. It was too good to be true!

Matthew asked, "Lord, are you really here?"

Jesus laughed. "I know what will help you believe. What do you have there on the table to eat?" James handed him a piece of fish. Jesus ate it, and then he said, "There. That proves I'm not a ghost!"

By now the disciples were convinced. They were so happy. Jesus was alive!

"Listen," Jesus said. "You've all seen what God has done. You are my witnesses. Now I want you to go and tell others."

He looked at Peter. "Remember when you were fishing with your nets, and I said I was going to show you how to catch people?" Peter nodded, and Jesus smiled.

"Good. That's what I want you all to do. Go fishing for people! Help them become disciples, just like you. Baptize them. Tell them what I've told you, and teach them to obey me."

MORE GEMS

Proclaim the good news.
—Luke 4:43

Preach the gospel.
—Mark 16:15

Fish for people.
—Matthew 4:19

Be filled with the Spirit.

—Ephesians 5:18

The Holy Spirit Comes

John 14:15–31; 15:26–27; 16:12–15; Acts 1:1–14; Luke 24:50–53; Mark 16:19–20; Acts 2:1–47

After Jesus died and rose again, he visited his disciples many times.

One afternoon, he ate a meal with them near the village of Bethany. After the meal, Jesus stood up to talk.

"Don't start making other disciples yet," he said. "First, God will send you a special gift. Wait until you get it."

"What is it, Lord?" Mark asked.

Jesus replied, "Do you remember how my cousin John baptized people with water?"

The disciples nodded.

"God is going to baptize you with the Holy Spirit," Jesus said. "He will give you power. Then you'll be strong enough and brave enough to tell others about me. That's when I want you to start sharing my good news with people. Begin in Jerusalem. Then go all through the country. Then go to the next country. And don't stop there! Keep going, all over the world."

Lifting his hands to bless his disciples, Jesus rose into the air.

The disciples were amazed. They watched him rise higher and higher. When they realized he was leaving, they were sad. But Jesus promised he would always be with them, even if they couldn't see him. They knew he would keep his promise.

A shining cloud appeared in the sky, and Jesus went up into it.

"I can't see him anymore!" said Matthew.

The disciples stood there, looking up. Then two angels appeared next to them. One angel said, "Don't worry. Jesus will come back someday."

Suddenly, the disciples weren't sad at all. They were joyful! Jesus had gone to heaven. He was still alive, and he would stay alive forever.

The disciples wanted to tell everyone the good news about Jesus and forgiveness for sin.

But first they had to wait for God's gift.

God's gift arrived on a holiday called Pentecost. Jews from all over the world had come to Jerusalem for a feast.

The disciples were staying at a friend's house when they heard a loud wind. Fire came down from heaven and landed on each of them. But it didn't burn them. It was the Holy Spirit. They started praising God in different languages.

People gathered outside the house. "What's happening?" they asked.

Peter told the crowd, "God is filling us with his Spirit, as he promised long ago." Then he said, "Jesus performed many miracles, proving he was God's Son. You and your leaders told the Romans to kill him, but God raised him from the dead."

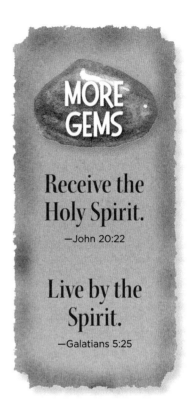

MORE GEMS

Receive the Holy Spirit.
—John 20:22

Live by the Spirit.
—Galatians 5:25

The people were very sorry for what they had done. They asked, "What should we do now?"

"Turn away from your sins and be baptized," Peter replied. "Your sins will be forgiven, and you'll be filled with the Holy Spirit."

It was the first time Peter told anyone God's good news. And that day, three thousand people were baptized and became followers of Jesus. Each one received God's special gift of the Holy Spirit.

Jesus Christ is Lord.

—Philippians 2:11

Saul Meets Jesus and Believes

Acts 9:1-20

Saul was an important Jewish leader who was very loyal to God. He obeyed all of God's rules, and he wanted other people to obey them too.

He had heard of Jesus. But Saul didn't believe Jesus was God's Son. He thought anyone who followed Jesus was disobeying God. So Saul went around arresting Jesus's followers and putting them in jail.

One day, Saul and some other men were traveling along a road to the city of Damascus. Suddenly, Saul saw a blazing light. It was so bright that he fell to the ground. Looking up, he tried to shield his eyes.

A voice asked him, "Why are you fighting against me?"

"Who are you?" Saul replied, his voice shaking with fear.

"I am Jesus. You've been causing trouble for my followers. When you do that, you're fighting against me."

Jesus told Saul to go to Damascus and wait. Then the bright light went away.

When Saul stood up, he couldn't see anything. The other men held his hand and led him to the city.

Saul stayed in a house there. For three days, he didn't eat or drink anything. Instead, he prayed and waited for Jesus to tell him what to do next.

Then a man named Ananias came to the house. Putting his hands on Saul's shoulders, Ananias said, "Jesus sent me to you so God will heal your eyes and fill you with his Spirit." Right away, Saul could see again. Ananias baptized Saul, and Saul received the gift of the Holy Spirit.

Saul was still very loyal to God. But now he believed Jesus was God's Son—the Lord of all the earth. He believed God had sent Jesus to save the world.

Best of all, the Holy Spirit was now living in Saul.

Saul had changed so much that he became known by another name—Paul.

Paul traveled to many cities and countries, telling people about God's kingdom and God's plan to save the world. "If you want to be saved," Paul said, "you must believe Jesus is Lord."

MORE GEMS

Revere Christ as Lord.
—1 Peter 3:15

His kingdom will never end.
—Luke 1:33

Believe in the Lord Jesus.
—Acts 16:31

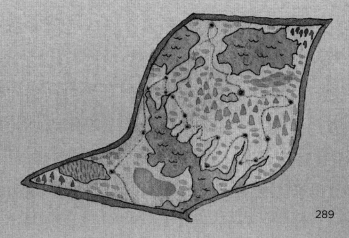

Do everything in love.

—1 Corinthians 16:14

Tabitha Helps People in Need

Acts 9:36–43

Tabitha lived in the town of Joppa. She believed in Jesus and loved him. Jesus had told his disciples, "If you love me, do what I say." So Tabitha loved her neighbors like Jesus said.

There were some poor widows in Tabitha's town. They needed food and warm clothes, but they didn't have money to buy those things.

Tabitha wanted to help these women and show them God's love. So she cooked stew and took it to them. She made robes for them to wear.

The widows were so thankful for Tabitha's help. They knew Tabitha loved them. And they loved her too.

One day, the widows heard some bad news. Tabitha was sick. They went to her home to see her. They wished they could do something to help her. At least they could try to cheer her up.

But Tabitha was too sick to eat. She was too sick to even talk.

As days passed, the women kept visiting her. Tabitha got worse, and the women grew more and more afraid.

Then came the worst news of all. Tabitha had died!
The widows bowed their heads and wept.

Some of their friends heard that Peter was visiting nearby. So they sent for him. They had faith in Jesus. They believed that God raised Jesus from the dead, and they hoped God would raise Tabitha too.

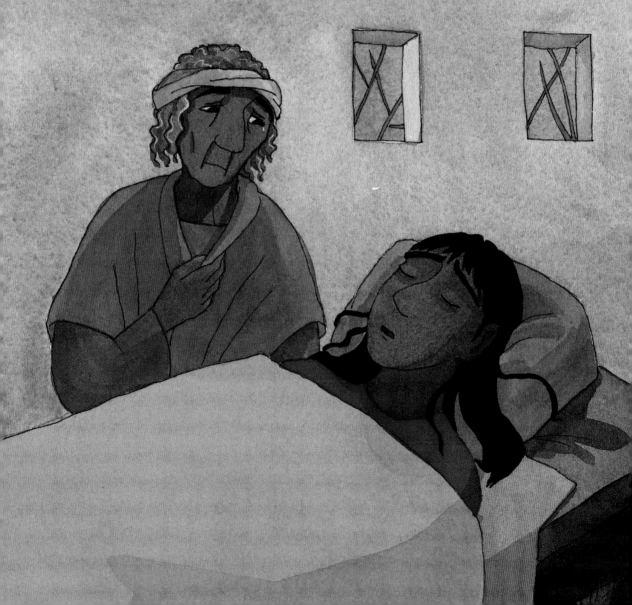

Peter arrived at Tabitha's house and went up to the room where she was lying. The women said, "Oh, Peter, please help her! She was always helping us. Look at these clothes she made!"

Peter saw how much they loved Tabitha. He knew she was a faithful disciple of Jesus. "Please leave the room," he told everybody. "I'll pray for her."

They all left, and Peter knelt and prayed. Then he said, "Tabitha, get up." Opening her eyes, she sat up. Peter helped her out of bed, then called for everyone to come back.

"Here she is!" he said, smiling.

The widows were so happy. Tabitha was alive! They hugged her and cried tears of joy.

The next day, Tabitha got right back to work doing good deeds and showing God's love.

MORE GEMS

Be kind and compassionate.
—Ephesians 4:32

Be rich in good deeds.
—1 Timothy 6:18

Christ's love compels us.
—2 Corinthians 5:14

Sing praises to God.

—Psalm 47:6

Two Prisoners Sing Praise Songs

Acts 16:16–40

Paul went to the city of Philippi with a man named Silas. Silas wanted to help Paul tell people about Jesus.

Some of the people believed their message. But a few men didn't like what they were doing, so they sent Paul and Silas to jail.

Soldiers locked chains on their hands and clamped blocks of wood on their feet. Paul and Silas could barely move.

But there were two things they could do. They could still pray. And they could still worship God.

So that's what Paul and Silas did. Sitting in jail, they prayed together and sang songs of praise. The other prisoners were surprised to hear that!

297

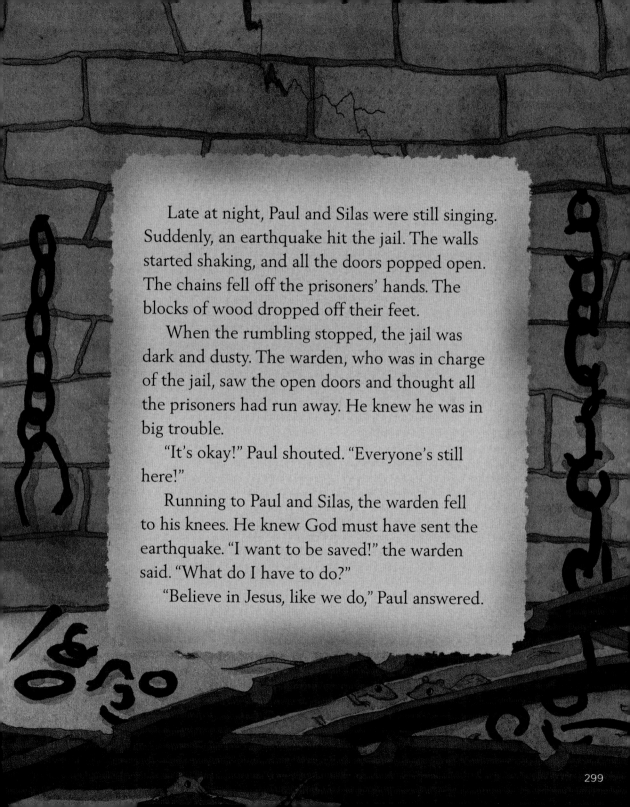

Late at night, Paul and Silas were still singing. Suddenly, an earthquake hit the jail. The walls started shaking, and all the doors popped open. The chains fell off the prisoners' hands. The blocks of wood dropped off their feet.

When the rumbling stopped, the jail was dark and dusty. The warden, who was in charge of the jail, saw the open doors and thought all the prisoners had run away. He knew he was in big trouble.

"It's okay!" Paul shouted. "Everyone's still here!"

Running to Paul and Silas, the warden fell to his knees. He knew God must have sent the earthquake. "I want to be saved!" the warden said. "What do I have to do?"

"Believe in Jesus, like we do," Paul answered.

Paul and Silas told the warden about Jesus. They said Jesus was God's Son, and he had come to give God's forgiveness to everyone who believed in him.

The warden was so thankful for this good news that he took Paul and Silas to his house. That night, the warden and his whole family put their faith in Jesus. Then Paul and Silas baptized them.

"Please, stay and eat with us," the warden said. He led Paul and Silas to the table. Everyone was smiling—the home was full of joy! And they all sang praises to God.

MORE GEMS

Praise God's name.
—Psalm 69:30

Sing joyfully to the LORD.
—Psalm 33:1

Rejoice in the Lord always.
—Philippians 4:4

Keep up your courage.

—Acts 27:25

Paul's Ship Hits a Storm

Acts 27; 2 Corinthians 11:25

When Paul was in Jerusalem, some men said he had broken the law, and he was arrested. A Roman centurion named Julius put Paul on a ship with other prisoners to take them to Rome. When everyone was on board, the captain of the ship yelled, "Untie the ropes, so we can get moving!"

As the ship pulled away from the pier, the sailors raised the sails. The sails caught the wind, and the captain steered the ship out to sea.

Everything went well for a while. But then the ship ran into a storm.

The wind and waves battered the ship, and the captain wrestled to keep it on course. "This wind is too strong!" he told Julius. "It's pushing us in the wrong direction." Julius tried to help him steer, but it was no use. So they gave up and let the ship go with the wind.

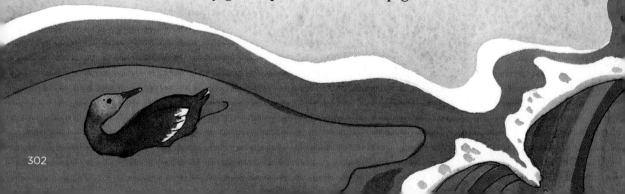

The storm raged all night. In the morning, the captain was afraid his ship would sink. They needed to make the ship lighter. "Get rid of everything we don't need!" he ordered. Paul and the other men threw all the cargo over the rails.

For days the storm tossed the ship around. "I don't know which way we're going," the captain told Julius. "We can't see the sun or the stars." The men began to lose hope.

Paul stood up and said, "Listen, everyone! Last night God told me we'd make it through this storm. He wants me to go to Rome to tell people about Jesus. I have faith in God, and I believe what he says. Keep up your courage, and don't lose heart!"

The next morning, one of the sailors called out, "Land! I see land!"

"This is our chance," said the captain. He steered the ship straight at the island. But before they reached shore, the bottom of the ship hit a sandbar. The ship was stuck.

The waves started to break up the back of the ship. Julius and Paul helped the others jump overboard, then leaped into the water. Some of the men grabbed pieces of wood that had fallen off the ship. Swimming, floating, paddling, and drifting, everyone made it safely to shore.

As Paul stood on the sand, he praised God for giving them hope and courage, and getting them through the storm.

MORE GEMS

Be strong and courageous.
—Deuteronomy 31:6

Hope in the LORD.
—Psalm 37:34

In God I trust.
—Psalm 56:11

Worship God!

—Revelation 19:10

John Sees God and Jesus in Heaven

Revelation 1:9–10; 4:1–5:14; 7:9–12; 19:9–10; 21:1–22:5; 22:8–9

One of Jesus's disciples, John, was living on the island of Patmos. As he was praying, he saw a door open in the sky. Then he heard a voice say, "Come up here, John. I'll show you what will happen in the future." The next thing John knew, he was in heaven. He saw God's throne, and he saw Jesus standing beside it.

John was in awe, but he wasn't afraid. God looked majestic, powerful, and holy but also gentle, kind, and good. John felt only great respect and love.

All kinds of people, from every nation of the world, were standing in front of God's throne. And thousands and thousands of angels were hovering in the air.

All the people and angels were worshiping God, praising him
for his goodness and thanking him for his awesome deeds.

"We praise you, God! We praise you, Jesus!"

John gazed around. Heaven and earth looked brand-new. He saw
a marvelous city—the new Jerusalem. And he heard God say, "Now
I will live with my people. They'll belong to me, and I'll belong to
them. No more death, no more pain, no more crying. I'm making
everything right; I'm making everything new!"

An angel took John to see the city up close. It glittered like a
jewel. The buildings were pure gold, and so was the main street.
The wall of the city was made of polished green stone, and it had
twelve white gates, each made of pearl. The bottom of the wall was
decorated with gemstones.

MORE GEMS

Worship the
LORD with
gladness.
—Psalm 100:2

Glorify the
King of heaven.
—Daniel 4:37

Then the angel showed John a crystal-clear river, flowing with the water of life. It came from God's throne and ran right through the city. Trees grew on both sides of the river, and each was a tree of life. "The trees always have fruit," the angel told John. "And their leaves have the power to heal people."

Heaven was amazing, and the angel was glorious. John bowed at his feet to worship him. Smiling, the angel said, "No, no, I'm a servant of the Lord, just like you. Don't worship me. Worship God!"

The Lord's coming is near.

—James 5:8

Jesus Promises to Come Back

Luke 12:35-48; John 14:1-3; Revelation 3:20; 22:12-21

On the day John visited heaven, Jesus spoke to him.

Standing next to God's throne, Jesus said, "Tell people I want them to invite me into their lives. I want them to let me into their hearts. It's like I'm waiting outside their house, knocking on their door and calling their name. If they open the door, I'll come in."

Jesus told John, "Explain to everyone that I'm offering them a gift. It's like people are dying of thirst, and I have a deep well of pure, fresh water. My water doesn't cost anything—it's free! They just have to come to me and take it. And when people drink my water, they'll be joyfully, truly alive. They won't get thirsty anymore, because I'll always have more for them."

John remembered something Jesus had told him and the other disciples. "Be ready, because you don't know when I'll come back," Jesus had said. "It's like I'm a house owner leaving on a trip, and my servants don't know how long I'll be gone. But they know I'll reward them if they're ready for me when I return, no matter what time of day or night that is. I want you all to be like that. Be ready!"

Putting his hand on John's shoulder, Jesus said, "I'm coming back, I promise. And I'm coming back soon."

John saw the love in Jesus's eyes. "Yes, Lord," he replied. "Please, come quickly!"

When John was back on the island of Patmos, he wrote down everything he had seen and heard in heaven. It was important to tell everyone what was going to happen. God wanted everybody to believe in Jesus, so that someday God and his people could live together forever.

We are God's children.

—Romans 8:16